## Life is Good, Post Stroke:
# I Am Now Better Not Bitter

Life is Good, Post Stroke: I Am Now Better Not Bitter
Copyright © 2023 by Leroy McClure Jr.

Published in the United States of America

ISBN   Paperback:    979-8-89091-230-5
ISBN   Hardback:     979-8-89091-231-2
ISBN   eBook:        979-8-89091-232-9

All rights reserved. No part of this publication may be reproduced, stored in a retrieval system or transmitted in any way by any means, electronic, mechanical, photocopy, recording or otherwise without the prior permission of the author except as provided by USA copyright law.

The opinions expressed by the author are not necessarily those of ReadersMagnet, LLC.

ReadersMagnet, LLC
10620 Treena Street, Suite 230 | San Diego, California, 92131 USA
1.619. 354. 2643 | www.readersmagnet.com

Book design copyright © 2023 by ReadersMagnet, LLC. All rights reserved.

Cover design by Ericka Obando
Interior design by Don De Guzman

Life is Good, Post Stroke:
# I Am Now Better Not Bitter

## Leroy McClure Jr.

# A NOTE TO THE READER

The author and editors have made every effort to ensure that the information contained in this book is accurate and complete. However, neither the publisher nor the author are medical professionals; therefore, they are not recommending medical services or providing professional medical advice to the individual reader. This book contains the author's personal experience with services, procedures, treatment, recovery, and healing due to a stroke. For your personalized healthcare or someone you may know, you must consult with your medical professional to recommend and supervise your medical journey. Neither the author nor the publisher shall be liable or responsible for any damage, injury, or loss damage allegedly arising from any information or ideas in this book.

## Scripture References

Unless otherwise noted, Scripture quotations are from the Holy Bible, NIV, New International Version, copyright © 1973, 1978, 1984, 2011 by International Bible Society.

**Photo by:** Rod Jones Photography

**Other books by Leroy McClure Jr.**

The Shot Doctor: Nothin' But Net

Why Sammy Still Can't Read: A Service Delivery Model for Creating a Culture of Reading

# ACKNOWLEDGMENT

This book is dedicated to the memory of my father, Leroy McClure Sr., and my mother, Marion Louise McClure. Their love for God and love for people has been the greatest influence on my life.

# CONTENTS

A Note to the Reader......................................................................v
Acknowledgment ........................................................................vii
Preface..........................................................................................1
Introduction.................................................................................4
Chapter 1:   48 Hours in Crisis ....................................................6
Chapter 2:   21 Days in NCCU ..................................................15
Chapter 3:   Different Strokes for Different Folks .......................34
Chapter 4:   Loving. Healthy. Recovery. .....................................43
Chapter 5:   Leroy's Walking Club ..............................................55
Chapter 6:   Can't Hurry Healing – FaceBook Posts...................67
Chapter 7:   On The Road and Driving Again ...........................82
Chapter 8:   Milestones Something Worth Talking About............96
Chapter 9:   The New Journey of Life .......................................103
Chapter 10: A New Theme: Better Not Bitter...........................109
References .................................................................................114

# PREFACE

Attitude

"The longer I live, the more I realize the impact of attitude on life. Attitude, to me, is more important than facts. It is more important than the past, than education, than money, than circumstances, than failures, than successes, than what other people think, say or do. It is more important than appearance, giftedness or skill. It will make or break a company...a church...a home. The remarkable thing is we have a choice every day regarding the attitude we embrace for that day. We cannot change our past. We cannot change the fact that people will act in a certain way. We cannot change the inevitable. The only thing we can do is play the one string we have, and that is our attitude. I am convinced that life is 10% what happens to me and 90% how I react to it.

And so it is with you...we are in charge of our Attitudes." (Swindoll 2022)

On July 30, 2021, my life changed forever. When I was in therapy after having a stroke, I knew that my attitude would have a direct correlation to my recovery. I told all of my therapists and counselors that my goal was to be the best patient I could be.

# PREFACE

When I was a child, two of my great uncles died from a heat stroke. I believe these men were in their 50's. In our family, it was imperative for the children to stay out of the sun or to make certain we wore a hat when we were in the sun. This was my first encounter with a stroke. As I got older, I later discovered that too much stress, eating poorly and not taking care of your body also contributed to having a stroke. I made up my mind to keep my body in good shape by eating the right food and exercising. I was determined to do all I could to avoid having a stroke.

Historically, my family have dealt with health issues, including obesity for a long time. Even though I have been an athlete my entire life, my health has always been a top priority especially after I quit playing basketball. I went to the gym five days a week. I always stayed in good shape because I kept my eyes on my weight and on what I was eating. I was committed to working out daily. After my basketball days were over, I started jogging until I was 50 something and then I replaced it with walking. I started walking up to eight miles a day. During my walk, I would do two to three thousand crunches while walking and one thousand pushups during those 2 ½ hours as I walked (10 sets of 100). I did this routine two to three times a week. The other two to three days I was in the gym lifting weights. This was my routine for over thirty years or until I was 61-years-old.

There comes a time in life when we must face the truth. Maybe it's now or maybe it's later when we become old. To be honest, in our later years of life the truth can be ambiguous at best. Since my stroke, the truth can be my life may never be normal again and I'm ready to accept this. I had to learn how to walk again and I no longer have that pep in my step, or I must learn how to run again and I don't move as fast as I used to move. If the truth be told, I'm not sure if what I'm experiencing come from old age or from my stroke.

However, what I do know is the obvious truth. Despite all the work I put into keeping my body in good shape, I had a stroke on July 30, 2021 in the gym when I was 61-years-old. My stroke was an arteriovenous malformation (AVM), a birth defect I didn't know about. None of my health preparations could have avoided the inevitable. I am on top of earth instead of earth on top of me. I am still alive to experience life and live life more abundantly.

It's time to share my testimony to all people that could be a stroke victim. I stand on the scripture that says to whom much is given, much is required. I had a minor setback for a major comeback. I can't hide my miraculous recovery under a basket. As I share my story, God will receive the glory. Romans 1:16 says, I am not a shame of the gospel because God's power brings salvation to all of those that believe. (NIV 2011)

Strokes are a leading cause of death in the United States with nearly 800,000 people having one each year. On average, a stroke occurs every 40 seconds in our country, according to the National Institute of Neurological Disorders and Stroke. Unfortunately, life sometimes leaves you bitter, you must believe with God's help, it will get better, better and better.

I don't understand all of what God is doing in my life; therefore, I will walk by faith. Perfect understanding will only come when I get to heaven. Through it all, I have learned to put my faith in Jesus and I have learned to depend upon God's word.

I truly stand on Romans 8:28 that says that "all things work together for the good of those that love the Lord and called according to His purpose." (NIV 2011) Despite all the knowledge and expertise I had prior to my setback, I knew my attitude would determine my comeback. As a leader experiencing life-altering adversity, I first swallowed my pride and then I learned how to become a good soldier.

# INTRODUCTION

Life as I knew it had instantly changed; therefore, I had to come to terms and grip with getting well. Had it not been for my faith and my relationship with Jesus Christ as my Lord and Savior, I could not have even imagine getting through this illness. We all begin to lean on the Lord and not our own understanding.

During my stroke, my faith grew even stronger. Laying on my back in NCCU for 21 days, I had plenty of time to reflect on scriptures. There are four scriptures mentioned throughout this book that helped me to transition from being a vibrant 61-year-old man to helplessly laying in a bed waiting for people to help me urinate, feed me and walk. Also, they put all kinds of tubes in my body filled with morphine among many other medicines to take the edge off a headache that wouldn't stop until the blood dissipated off my brain. In addition, the scriptures strengthened me as I was confined to a wheelchair for 10 weeks.

The first scripture was from John 10:10, "The thief comes only to steal and kill and destroy; I have come that they may have life, and have it to the full." The abundant life does not mean wealth, safety, or status. In fact, it means, means "exceedingly, very highly, beyond measure...." The abundant life means a continual process of learning, practicing, and maturing, as well as failing, recovering, enduring, and overcoming, because in our present life, our present state, we see but a poor reflection, as in a mirror. (Rodgers 2022)

Second, James 2:20 says, "You foolish person, do you want evidence that faith without works is dead?" (NIV 2011) Once we trust Jesus as Lord and Savior in our hearts by the power of the Holy

Spirit, He transforms us. We are then saved to do good works on the earth. Our deeds are the outer reflection of the inward transformation.

Third, God allows painful situations so that He can reconcile us to Himself. The verse from Romans 8:28 says that, "And we know that in all things God works for the good of those who love Him, who have been called according to His purpose." (NIV 2011) And what that means is that both good and bad, pleasant and unpleasant, everything and that includes every person that works together for the best. For those who love God, everything that we meet in life, everything, without exception, works together for our best.

Finally, Hebrews 11:6 says, "But without faith, it is impossible to please Him, for he who comes to God must believe that He is, and that He is a rewarder of those who diligently seek Him." (NIV 2011) This scripture means we keep seeking God until we find Him, not resting until we hear from Him in our situation or circumstance. Doing something "diligently" means doing it energetically and persistently.

I have quoted these verses through every step of my recovery and adjusting to a new normal. I'm so grateful to the administrators, doctors, nurses, and other staff at Methodist Charlton Medical Center and Methodist Dallas Medical Center [Methodist Brain and Spine Institute/Neuro Critical Care Unit] (Dallas, TX), Encompass Health Rehabilitation Hospital (Arlington, TX), and Centre for Neuro Skills (Irving, TX) for being a bridge to a meaningful recovery. I praise God daily for my healing.

These healthcare providers, expert neurosurgeons, and support from my wife, adult children, extended family members, and friends have added value to my life with incredible love and care. The next chapters in this book gives you a glimpse into my life of living with a stroke and eagerness to openly share my personal journey in real life.

# CHAPTER 1

Lifting weights in the gym 3 days before my stroke (July 27, 2021).

## A Stroke in the Gym

On July 30, 2021, my family and I experienced a life-changing event. As a virile, energetic and in excellent shape, my life changed in just a blink of an eye during my early morning workout routine, which was something that I have done for more than 30 plus years. With an excruciating headache and slurred speech, it was time for a 911 call for medical help before it was too late. At that moment, I was alive. I didn't even ponder the thought that my life would be changed forever. In fact, I was in the gym at Fitness Connection when it happened. I remember it so clearly. I was on one of the machines and I was almost done with my work out for the day. I had one more set; therefore, I increased the weight. It was so heavy that when I finished, my head started aching. I saw a friend of mine passing by me. I stopped him and said, "Hey man, follow me as I go to the water fountain." He followed me and the headache continued. As I was drinking water, my speech started slurring. Then I told him to call 911. The paramedics came and took me to Methodist Charlton Hospital and then they care-flighted me to Methodist Dallas Hospital.

Puzzled. Bewildered. Confused. I needed my wife, Yvette, who I had dropped off in Shreveport, Louisiana on Wednesday, July28, 2021 so that she could travel to Little Rock, Arkansas on Saturday, July 31, 2021 to stay with her sister, Monica. Exactly a week ago on July 23, 2021, my wife's sister had a series of mini strokes due to her heart condition called Atrial fibrillation (AFib), which was shooting blood clots to her brain for a week. She went into the hospital on the Friday unable to walk and to talk. With massive prayers, she was discharged from the hospital two days later on Sunday walking and talking.

I am grateful for my sister-in-law's outcome being very quick to return home and getting some therapy. Based on the bleeding on my brain, I am so thankful that some of my old acquaintances and friends acted responsibly and quickly to get help for me. My friend, looked through my phone and called my youngest daughter, Princes who immediately called my wife between the tears, sobs and confusion of what was going on with me, her dad. Princess immediately contacted my wife who quieted her down to try to understand what was going on. My wife gave our daughter a power of attorney to make medical decisions in her absence. My wife gave the phone to her younger sister and ran to grab her suitcases to head back to Dallas as quickly as the car could travel.

My wife prayed, talked to as many people who could help her understand what was going on. Our oldest daughter had arrived at the hospital and they gave a slip of paper with a definition of arteriovenous malformation (AVM). I had been diagnosed with AVM, a brain illness that I didn't know that I had.

A vessel was leaking on the tissue of the brain in the cerebellum, which is located at the back part of the brain. The bleeding of the brain was causing a level 3 headache. During the CT scan and other tests, the doctors concluded that this was a serious stroke and they could not treat it at their location. I would have to be care-flighted to their main hospital in mid-town Dallas, Texas. I had no clue as to what to expect and neither did my wife and our four adult children ranging in ages 23 to 39.

Questions popped into my mind. How long will it take my wife to get to the hospital to make sense of all of this? What would be the changes in my life after a stroke? How would it affect my family, my work, and others? What part of the brain was affected? How badly was my brain injured?

## I Need Yvette

All I could think of was when will my wife get here! I knew that as soon as she found out about me, she would be back home to help me get through my stroke. I was not going to feel safe or have any peace until I saw her face. I knew with her being there, she would do everything there is to do to make certain that I was well taken care of. Oh yeah, I have confidence in her but I have more confidence in God using her during a time like this. My two daughters were there and kept me updated on Yvette's whereabouts and her arrival. Once she arrived, I was able to let go and let God. After being married to her for more than 25 years, I knew she would make certain with God's help, I get the best healthcare the hospital could provide. If the healthcare had been insufficient, she would have gotten me to the Mayo Clinic in Rochester, Minnesota since we had a previous relationship with them when my son was a patient.

Once the news traveled to relatives and friends all over the country, my cell phone was full every single hour. The nurses would not let me even touch the cell phone. Then my wife had a brilliant idea-keep a daily journal and send information out to all of our family and friends, and she even created a note to share with our children and close relatives who had an iPhone. The updates helped limit the visitors because the COVID-19 hospital restrictions were in effect during this time where only the same two visitors per day were allowed in the room from 7:00 a.m. to 7:00 p.m. This daily update helped my family and friends to better understand the process and procedures for dealing with AVM and my wife to keep her sanity.

The following section gives you real-time encounters of the unknown experience of an AVM stroke. The snippets are mostly things I did not witness nor remember; however, my wife captured intimate details as she wrote in her journal all events happening in my stroke life. Her writings depict my medical journey from the day I had my stroke to the end of my stay in NCCU.

## Yvette's Text Journal Messages

Life, as I knew it had instantly changed; therefore, I had to come to terms and grip with the reality of the unknown. According to my wife, I spent three weeks fighting for my life at Methodist Dallas Neurocritical Care Unit (NCCU).

Yvette's Journal served as a daily post of how the hand of God moved on my health condition. The daily updates consist of the times that critical care was provided followed by prayer requests and answered prayers.

## July 30, 2021: God's Favor – The right place at the right time

**9am-10am:** *Leroy was working out at the gym and his right lip dropped. He said he lifted too much weights and felt something pop or pulled in his head. His speech sounded like he was inebriated (a drunk person). He went over to a friend of his and they immediately called 911. He was transported to the hospital by an ambulance.*

**11am:** *I received a call from our daughter, Princess who informed me that their dad was rushed to the hospital due to a possible stroke. I was in Louisiana helping my sister with her events liquidation sale and the next day I would be headed to Little Rock, Arkansas to take care of my sister who had a stroke exactly a week before my husband on July 23, 2021. I packed my bags and my sister, Chaundra, and my brother, Andre drove me to Dallas in 2 hours 15 minutes of usually a 3-hour drive. Princess went to the hospital immediately. On the drive, I gave Princess a medical power of attorney for her dad in my absence to make decisions for the treatment of her dad. Our daughter, Jenna and our son, King came, too. Leroy's sister, Elaine met our adult children there.*

**12pm:** *A CT scan was performed at Methodist Charlton Hospital (MCH). The computerized tomography (CT) scan revealed that Leroy had a leak in a vessel located in the cerebellum (back part of the brain) due to a rare birth defect called arteriovenous malformation (AVM). This is considered a hemorrhaging stroke. Leroy has never had a symptom or been to the doctor for any illness such as diabetes, AFib, or high blood pressure, the typical contributing factors of some strokes. This was an unknown illness at best. This was on the scale of our son, King, who has Hypertrophic cardiomyopathy (HCM). No symptoms, no illness or contributing factors for the first life changing event in our lives (please see Chapter 3 for this story).*

**Diagnosis:** *Leroy has tangled blood vessels in the cerebellum part of the brain (small area in the back of the head.) The brain disorder is called AVM. It is a rare brain disorder from birth. It is not hereditary. You can go all of your life and not know that you have this brain defect. It causes severe headaches and seizures. Also, you* have speech issues making you sound like a drunk person, problem swallowing, sensitive to light, nausea, etc. The bright side, you can live a long life if the AVM's blood vessels don't develop an aneurysm.

The tangled vessels have to be tracked down because there is a leakage or one that has possibly ruptured. This is done through an angiogram and embolization of the vessels. Initially, his head was hurting him really bad. It was a level 10. His blood pressure was high. He was given morphine every 2 hours.

***1pm-2pm:*** Leroy was care-flighted from Methodist Charlton Hospital (MCH) to its sister hospital, Methodist Dallas Medical Center [Methodist Brain and Spine Institute/Neuro Critical Care Unit] (NCCU). They had received the CT scan performed by a Neurologist at Methodist Charlton Hospital.

***3pm:*** I made it to Methodist Dallas Hospital. I couldn't go see Leroy because his sister, Elaine, and our daughter, Jenna, were in his room. Only the same two people each 24-hour period was allowed in the room due to COVID-19 protocol.

I was not allowed to go back to see him even as his wife. I dropped my head and prayed asking God to grant me favor to see and be with my husband.

***4:45pm-7pm:*** The Lord heard my cry. I was granted favor to see him for 10 minutes; however, it turned out that I was the only one with him until closing time at 7:00 pm. I spoke to the nurse to better understand what AVM was and began my Mayo Clinic research- what it is, what it does, where it comes from, etc. What are the next steps in the healing process?

***7pm:*** We all had to leave the hospital because of the spikes in COVID-19 cases. No one can spend the night.

***9pm:*** It's time to go the family's glass/wood round kitchen table to know how to scale the wall of this giant of an unknown sudden illness out of the pit of hell. Jenna came to the house to spend the night. We talked about the situation. Strategies to help in the process and first and foremost our spiritual warfare moves. Around 11:45pm, Leroy's four adult children and I prayed for him to experience no pain.

## Saturday, July 31, 2021: Oh no, Locks Cut Off!

***3am:*** *CT Scan performed. The bleeding had increased and water was on the brain.*

***7:39am:*** *Leroy's headache was a 2 out of 10 on the pain scale. God heard our cry.*

***9:30am:*** *Leroy was prepped for an angiogram to locate the leaky vessel. They wheeled him out and attempted to do an angiogram. God had a different plan.*

*Jenna and I began to pray for wisdom, open the doctor's eyes to see what to do. All of a sudden the doctor came out and said, "A change in plans!" Leroy kept complaining that he couldn't breathe. The reason for the non-breathing was because the water on the brain had increased since yesterday. The water on the brain is called Hydrocephalus, which is a build-up of fluid in the cavities deep within the brain. It has meningitis type symptoms restricting the breathing, swallowing and the speech.*

***11am:*** *The doctors cleared the room to put a shunt in his front lobe of the brain to drain the fluid off the brain. The goal is to see clear fluid and no red blood in the drainage. No blood represents that the leakage has stopped. The doctors had to shave the front part of Leroy's hair locks to implant the shunt in the front part of the brain. Jenna remarked, "Oh no! If this was my husband who has massive locks had to do this, he would rather die." I replied, "I am cutting your dad's locks so he can live."*

***2:00pm:*** *He worked with speech therapist. He was sitting up straight—alert, talkative, swallowed really good. Leroy said he liked sitting up.*

***3:05pm:*** *Underwent an MRI of the brain just to see if they missed anything on the CT Scan.*

***3:30pm-4:45pm:*** *Leroy slept off and on.*

***5pm-7pm:*** *The nurse managed the minimal headache pain. He had a good several hours.*

## Sunday, August 1, 2021: A New Day, A New Twist

*Today, I was attacked in my sleep with a different type of headache, nausea and my eye feeling strangely. I started praying through the power of the Holy Spirit. I reached out to Jenna and my brother, Gary, immediately to pray. I needed a direct line to Jesus through the Holy Spirit praying. I know the enemy was trying to send me to the hospital on my own stretcher. I battled through JESUS, JESUS, JESUS strong and mighty name. I showered and got dressed in record time. I got to the hospital at 8:05am. I walked in while the doctor was checking Leroy and making his report. Here is the beginning of today's hand of God at work:*

**8:10am:** Neurocritical Care Physician proclaimed loudly and at least 3 times—he (Leroy) looks really good and he has made good progress. They ordered the angiogram for this morning. We have to keep him quiet, no talking so that the blood pressure stays at an abnormal but normal level so that the leaking vessel does not further rupture.

**10:30am:** We got the report from the MRI (3D image of the brain). The angiogram is scheduled for 12 noon.

**11:15am**: I started sending Prayer Request out.

**12:15pm:** We are still waiting for the team to cart Leroy off for his angiogram. All of a sudden, Leroy yelled for help because he felt a huge burst of pain with the headache pain reaching at least a 20. The vessel had ruptured and the blood was irritating the brain. He should have been in the procedure but a schedule issue occurred. THIS IS AN ATTACK OF THE ENEMY, I said!!!! Need the serious prayers now. In the name of Jesus, we bind the enemy up. We lose in the name of Jesus to open up the space and the Holy Spirit to finding this blood vessel and capping it off!!! They are draining blood now.

Only through God's grace that I have not passed out screaming at the top of my lungs!!! Work Holy Spirit! In the name of Jesus, I pray!!! Amen

**12:55pm:** I prayed with Leroy. He was taken to the area for the angiogram. Jenna and I rode on the patient elevator with him.

*Then we were escorted to the waiting room where Jenna and I slept, texted, zoomed with family (Yvette), and talked to only Leroy's adult children.*

*They finished the procedure at 5pm. It took so long because a vessel ruptured around 11:30am. They just told us to go back to the room and they will bring him back. Not saying how long that will take. Even if he hasn't returned back to the room at 7:00 pm, we will have to still leave the hospital. Just waiting. We asked God for the doctors to be careful, etc. While the waiting seems forever, we want them to take their time to do the procedure accurately and find the vessel and cap it off even if it takes all night.*

**5:10pm:** *Jenna and I became restless from sitting for four hours and not knowing what was going on with Leroy. No one came out to tell us what was going on with him. Jenna saw Leroy's nurse and asked him what was going on and why was it taking so long. The nurse said that we could go back up to the room because Leroy will be coming back up soon. We returned to the room as quickly as possible.*

**6:20pm:** *Nurses and orderlies rolled Leroy back into the room. The surgical team fixed up all of his tubes-feeding, dehydration, IVs and other medicines. They propped him up and began to do work with him. We are trusting God to hold the glue air-tight until His return to earth. He sure can do this. Who has the whole world in their hand? Yes, it is God. Next....*

*Once the vessel leading to the AVM burst, we knew we were in it for the long haul. Time went out the door. I pondered the thought that I was in critical condition and I was truly relying on God to comfort me, give me pace and ultimately heal me. The next three weeks lying in bed in NCCU had its series of roller-coaster bumps from losing the ability to really talk, swallowing and now walking. The ruptured vessel, the shunt and now an EVD machine hooked to both sides of my head/face to keep me from moving from left to right so that the fluid would drain the water/blood off my brain was my new found life-saving treatment. Interesting enough, I did not have time to recover from the first procedure on Sunday, August 1 before I was back on the table 48 hours later. The next chapter walks you through the medical treatment of the next critical stage of my struggle to recover and walk gain.*

## CHAPTER 2

# 21 Days in NCCU

**First Week in NCCU**
**Monday, August 2, 2021: Still Fighting-the Blood Won't Let Up**

*According to my wife, I spent three weeks fighting for my life in NCCU. My wife told me she felt as if she was in the major heavyweight fight without gloves. She recalls using the biblical story of Nehemiah, who was sent to rebuild the walls of Jerusalem. For Nehemiah, it was 52 days of a fight from fierce opposition. For my wife, she did not fight alone. She formed a team of pray warriors called "On the Wall." This group of family and friends would continue to pray fervently every day and where there is an emergency need over the next three weeks in NCCU. Her journal writing did not let up to family and friends.*

***6:30am:*** *I had a yelling and crying fit at Jesus' feet this morning. I just did not have the strength nor the desire to go on or to move. I was crying so hard I did not know what time it was because I was meeting with Leroy's siblings at 7:00 am by phone. I got up praying and went to Leroy's closet and fell to my knees and filled at least two huge buckets of tears. The telephone meeting was designed to update his siblings and display rumors that while their brother is in critical condition, doctors do not believe it is fatal nor is he in a vegetative state.*

***7:15am:*** *Had telephone meeting with Leroy's siblings to go over what is going on with him.*

**8am.** *I left home headed to the hospital. I need God's grace to be sufficient and me to really develop my language. I need a direct line to Jesus because of the decisions still ahead--work, finances, etc. The bread winner of the home will not work at least a year or two years.*

**8:15am:** *My brother called me and gave me a good word soldiers quote: When we are in battle, we are usually hunkered down in a foxhole. When one of us get low on ammunition, we say to the other, cover me while I reload. Did I need the covering!*

**8:45am:** *Walked in late to the hospital. The nurse said the early morning CT scan revealed blood still on brain after the procedure.*

**Update/Praise Report to Family and Friends**

*Good Morning Everyone: Like Nehemiah told Sanballat (Nehemiah 6:1-3), I'm not coming off this wall until my labor is done! Just got to the hospital. After getting the runaround, praying all the way.*

*We came into the room and the PT and OT ladies were working with him. They had helped him get out of bed, walk to the chair and set up in the recliner. They will let him sit up for one hour increments at different times. He took steps on his own with the use of a walker. He responds better sitting up than lying down. His blood pressure is now normal. More fluid has drained off the brain. No new blood coming from the brain just the old blood dripping out with the fluid. He ate a little. Now he has 7-Up to help absorb some of the fluid around the brain. His headache is a 2 out of 10. He will have a CT scan today. They keep saying he is really strong. The goal is getting him walking on his own with the recommendation of a new workout plan--three times a week for PT, OT, and speech therapy. The surgeon made his rounds and said he is progressing really good. He looks good and use of hands, arms and eyes are doing what they are supposed to be doing--working. All of these functions are right on track. He was given hydrocodone to help him sleep by taking the edge off the headache and to relax so that the brain continues to heal naturally with medicine.*

*Today, as God emptied me of me, I am able to see Leroy's physical state from a new level. I appreciate the baby steps from falling down, now crawling and Lord willing walking like he should. Praises to God for me to be a new wife with new appreciation for the man God has given me on earth. I feel you guys holding up my arms. Don't let me try to put them down. I love you all and so does Leroy and the kids.*

**10:05am:** *Leroy did have the CT scan early this morning. The nurse said she didn't and couldn't tell us the results.*

*The Internal Medicine doctor stopped by to introduce himself because when he gets out of NCCU, he will work to make sure Leroy's other body functions are working properly.*

*He revealed the results of the CT scan because he thought I knew. He revealed: there was new blood on the CT scan.*

*That is bad. It could mean that there is a new aneurysm vessel or the capping off of the main vessel did not work. I believe the sealing of the vessel worked. The neurosurgeon team is aware. They are in surgery right now. (10:40am)*

*When the Interventional Neuroradiology Physician, made his rounds he did not tell me about the findings from the CT scan report.*

**11:45am:** *I sent a text to our friend, who is a medical doctor about Leroy's procedure on Sunday.*

*Hi Friend: I was so overwhelmed last night because he got from the procedure at 6:20pm. It took 4 hours for the procedure.*

*We had to leave at 7:00 pm due to COVID-19 protocols. The Interventional Neuroradiology Physician told us the embolization worked to seal the vessel that leaked and it was the same vessel that ruptured at 12noon on yesterday while they were prepping him for the angiogram. They had to do a CT scan early this morning because after the procedure he put up a real fight with nurses which they say was due to the anesthesia medicine.*

*It took six male nurses/other personnel to lay him back down flat because he sat straight up. It was just symbolic of when Jesus went to the cross and died on Friday and rose up from the grave on Sunday.*

*Anyway, the early morning CT scan revealed blood still on the brain and draining in the bag. I am waiting for someone to tell me what this means. He is stable. No headaches, walked with a walker to a recliner where he has been since 9:00 am, ate food, talking, sleeping, brushed his own teeth, cognition is still on point, and his blood pressure has return to a good number (132). The fluid is still draining and the bag is clear. Earlier, the nurse saw a big clot of blood come through the fluid drain bag around and was stuck in the tube. Twenty minutes later, the clot broke into pieces and no other blood has come through the tube. The Interventional Neuroradiology Physician was in surgery and not able to answer questions nor attend to this new issue. My family members are holding up my arms. We are praying, praying, crying and crying. But like Nehemiah told Sanballat-I'm not coming off this wall until my labor is done. We still have to deal with the damaged AVM in about 6 weeks. I am in it for the long haul. I will keep you up to date on the situation. Thanks, we feel the prayers. Thanks* **(End of the text to a personal doctor friend)**

***1pm/1;30pm:*** *SSent second text to our doctor friend: The Interventional Neuroradiology Physician wants to go ahead and do surgery on the AVM area on tomorrow. It feels like I have been punched in the gut. If this is not asking too much, can I have a conversation with you and not texting? I am really trying to hold it together. Please at your earliest convenience, it will help me keep my sanity and composure. Thanks*

***5pm:*** *The Neurocritical Care Physician said the Interventional Neuroradiology Physician will re-enter the cerebellum to clean up or embolize the other vessels including flowing directly into the AVM. The Interventional Neuroradiology Physician will perform an Endovascular embolization through the angiogram procedure. The neurosurgeon came by and explained that he will use an "all-star" team to go back and embolize every vessel in the AVM. The other 6-8 doctors will be working on different aspects of the cerebellum's and AVM's vessels to ensure nothing is missed in this delicate procedure.*

**8pm:** *Call to my brother to get scriptures to pray over the doctors, Leroy and myself for the next surgery.*

**9pm:** *Had a FaceTime talk and prayer time with our four adult children.*

## Tuesday, August 3, 2021: Let's Do It Again

**8:10am:** *Arrived to Leroy's room. He was sitting in the recliner. He was restless last night. The nurse told me that his angiogram is for 10am.*

**8:30am:** *I started to quote tons of scriptures in Leroy's ear. He was in lots of pain, agitated, no bowel movement, not allowed to drink anything, blood pressure up all morning, etc. They could not give him any real strong pain medicines nor Morphine. He was uncomfortable in the bed. He sat up in the chair for about 1 hour 30 minutes.*

*The Neurocritical Care Physician came to the room to inform of the 10am schedule and what would happen during the process.*

**10:16am:** *Now the nurse just said 3:00 pm for the angiogram...hold the time loosely. It's about making sure they have the right team for this procedure...please help to keep standing up against the devil... he is a LIAR!*

**11am:** *Leroy is restless. They are managing his headache pain level--it was 10, now 2 to 4...they are sedating him moderately and very carefully. His spirits are good. He can't eat anything until after recovery. Last meal was about 6:00 pm on yesterday.*

**12:16pm:** *the time is pushed back to 4:30 pm now. I am still trusting God that every delay is in our favor! His time. His way. Romans 8:28 says, "And we know that all things work together for good to them that love God, to them who are called according to his purpose." (NIV 2011) I am holding on to God's promises!*

**4pm:** *The nurse informed us that the surgery team is ready for him to come down. I prayed over Leroy before we left for the procedure area. We traveled on the Trauma Elevator with Leroy to the pre-op area. Here we grow again.*

***4:45pm:*** *We had a pre-op meeting with the Interventional Neuroradiology Physician and prayed with him. Here is the prayer:*

FATHER, we thank you in the matchless name of JESUS for the miracles you are about to manifest before our very eyes.

We recognize that the battle is not ours, but yours LORD. We thank you that all we must do is stand on the promises that you have already spoken and see your salvation. We thank you that you are with us and we are not afraid. We know that you did not give us the spirit of fear, but of LOVE, POWER, and a SOUND mind. Dear GOD, we trust you with all our heart and lean not to our own understanding.

We thank you that you are leading this medical team that is taking care of our loved ones. We thank you that you are guiding them every step of the way and your will be done. If the enemy should try to steer them off the safest and most direct path to the corrective measures that you would breathe the right path into them.

We know that when the HOLY SPIRIT joins that team, you will lead them into all truth and the proper procedures. YOU will reveal to them all that is necessary to bring our loved ones back to the quality of life that you have for them. We know that the medical team has a plan, but you have the ultimate plan and the final say so. Order their steps LORD as you guide their hands, sharpen their vision, reveal the truth, and fill their hearts with compassion. Give them revelation and knowledge to follow you and perform the necessary procedures as never before. We know that you are a WAYMAKER, MIRACLE WORKER, LIGHT IN THE DARKNESS. Even when we don't see it, you are working it for our good. You said in your word that we should ask specifically for what we want from you. You told us to seek you while you may be found. Your word reassures us that if we are diligent in our seeking you to anoint and BLESS this medical staff to complete what you have allowed this medical team to discover. Your word says that you are a rewarder of those that diligently seek you with their whole heart. We are knocking at the door, and we speak healing and recovery over Leroy and Monica. We are speaking those things that are not as though *they were. We PRAISE your HOLY NAME for the wisdom that you have placed over this team and showing them what to do next. We know that you will always lead us and satisfy our heart's desires. YOUR righteousness has already paved the way. LORD we know that you are continually restoring Monica and Leroy's strength and they are going to spring up and their testimonies will be full. According to your word, we overcome by the BLOOD OF THE LAMB and the words of our testimonies. You will take us through places we have never been and change darkness to light, sickness to health and make all the rough ways smooth.*

*You will not abandon us. Even on our sick bed, you will give us strength and make us well. We are convinced that YOU who began this gracious work will faithfully continue it until the very day that CHRIST appears. FATHER, this is the confidence we have in you, that all that we have declared in your darling son JESUS's name, we know that you have heard our pleas and that you are already answering. And because we know you heard us; we know that you have given us the desires of our heart. Now unto HIM that is able to do EXCEEDINGLY ABUNDANTLY above all that we ask or think, keep us from falling and present us faultless before the FATHER, be GLORY, DOMINION and POWER FOREVERMORE. AMEN.*

*1 John 4:4 declares that "Greater is HE that is within thee than he that is in the world!"*

*The Interventional Neuroradiology Physician: the Interventional Neuroradiology Physician will go back into the cerebellum area and look at the large long line of vessels that go into the AVM. During the Sunday's procedure, the Interventional Neuroradiology Physician said there were a line of multiple aneurysms spots-in places of some of the vessel that they fixed with onyx. This was the same vessel that leaked and ruptured. There was no more leaking from vessels after the Sunday's angiogram.*

*The Interventional Neuroradiology Physician said that he would do the procedure with "care and caution". These were the exact words we used in our prayer on Sunday, July 31, 2021.*

After the conversation with the Interventional Neuroradiology Physician, I signed paperwork for surgery and anesthesia.

**5:30pm:** They wheeled Leroy back to the area where the procedure would be conducted. They had not started the anesthesia.

**8:45pm: UPDATE/TEXT OF PRAISE**

*Man puts on the bandage but God does the healing*

**8.3.21 UPDATE:** *The surgical procedure for Leroy was over at 8:30pm. The Interventional Neuroradiology Physician called me at 8:45pm. He and the God-selected team successfully attacked the vessels/veins to the AVM that could cause a fatal stroke only God would know the time. The other vessel that he shot Onyx to had many aneurysm parts throughout the vessel. He said that was finished off on Sunday. He was just re-inspecting it. There was no other vessel that had any abnormal or suspicious aneurysm parts at all. He has no new bleeding from Sunday other than from tonight's procedure. There is swelling and blood on the brain. They are watching this the next couple of days. He said Leroy got up literally fighting from the surgery. He said that was a really good sign. Now his speech, walking and headaches gets better as the brain resets and the blood/swelling goes down/away. All praises to our God! Thanks for covering us while we go through this most difficult journey! We really love you and appreciate you.*

## Wednesday, August 4, 2021: Loving Leroy to Good Health

**7am:** *Woke up during the night with stomach issue and under attack with a funny headache. Text Gary for prayer. It hits every now and then.*

**8:12am:** *Arrived in Leroy's hospital room. He gave Princess and I a thumbs up once he saw us. The night shift nurse report: He slept really good. No headache at all. The fluid bag still draining water with only new blood from last night's surgical procedure. They had to put a safety button on his bed because he actually tried to get out bed. He got to the end of the bed with his feet hanging out. No food yet. He is scheduled for a MRI and MRI-A.*

*AMAZING GOD!!!!*

***9:03am:*** *OT and PT therapists arrived for Leroy's therapy time. They will work with him five days a week. Leroy walked on a walker mostly pushing it himself with a little assistance from the OT/PT therapists. On the FaceTime: my mom, Chaundra, and Jenna watched him really walk.*

***9:27am:*** *The Interventional Neuroradiology Physician and Neurocritical Care Physician came by as Leroy was brushing his teeth and washing his face on his own. When he was walking, the fluid bag was not connected to him and his head started hurting. It was a pain threshold of 5.*

*The Interventional Neuroradiology Physician: The vessels to the AVM was embolized with the Onyx. They pose no threat or danger of leaking or aneurysm. Next step is to treat it with radiation to permanently kill those vessels. "We are praying off radiation, too," I remarked.*

*Neurocritical Care Physician: Ordered medicines for pain management and other bodily functions.*

*Pain Management after Walking*

*They are giving him the following medicines now with 7-Up to drink.*

- *Phedaphine-blood pressure*
- *Murilex-powder & Colase for bowel movements*
- *Pepsin-code stomach to prevent ulcers*
- *B12 shot*
- *Norco- pain pill for headache*

***10:30am-11:30am:*** *Leroy still sitting in the chair. He slept until time to eat.*

***11:45am:*** *He ate lunch. He had chicken, rice, fruit. Everything had to be cut up into fine pieces. He could use a fork really good. He can't control his chewing due to the blood on the brain. He gets tired chewing and the food isn't swallowed, which causes him to choke. He has to build up the mouth and throat muscles. Speech therapy helps with swallowing techniques as well as speaking using the throat and mouth muscles.*

***12:45pm-4:15pm:*** *Leroy slept a lot. He woke up around 4:15pm with a level 5 headache. He was administered pain medication. Still no bowel movement.*

***5:30pm:*** *The rehabilitation doctor came in to visit Leroy. When he is discharged, he will immediately go stay at a facility for three weeks. They will monitor his brain and surgery to ensure he rehabs and not get injured nor bleeds, etc. Leroy's headache is at a 3. He was nauseated. Seems like something was stuck in his throat. He was given Zofran in his IV and pain medicine as a shot in his arms.*

***5:40pm-7pm:*** *Leroy mostly slept. The headache was now a 5. They administered pain medicines. He ate dinner. The chicken was too tough to eat. I requested a soft diet for Leroy. He has no control over swallowing. He is using muscles that are being controlled by the area that is still full of blood. During the shift change around 6:50 pm, the nurse described to the night shift nurse that Leroy had a Cerebellum Hemorrhaging Stroke with Hydrocephalus due to the AVM. He had the embolization twice in a 48-hour period.*

## **Thursday, August 5, 2021: Moving into Long-Term Care**

*I had conversation with my brother as to how to stay on the wall without wavering. I needed words of encouragement because of the weariness and impatience with the healing process. We talked. We prayed. We were off the phone and fast asleep about 1:20am.*

***8:25am:*** *Arrived in Leroy's hospital room. Today it is King's day to stay with me. He was so happy to see King. He introduced him to the nurse.*

<u>*The nurse's overnight report sent to family and friends:*</u>

*Slept good. He had pain medicine throughout the night. They did not do the MRI and MRI-A. The fluid bag is still draining water with only new blood from Tuesday's surgical procedure. He tried to get out of the bed again to go to the bathroom. They already had put a safety button on his bed to notify the nurse if he gets out of the bed. He was not hungry. His pancakes and eggs getting colder.*

**9am:** *The OT and PT therapists came in for therapy session. Due to a headache, Leroy got out of bed to the recliner and walked in place. He brushed his teeth and washed his own face.*

**9:45am:** *The rehabilitation came in to visit Leroy. He recommended getting Leroy pain medicines that are specifically for nerves especially around the brain. The doctor gives the hospital orders for what the rehab should consist of for patients. The doctor ordered Gallaphentin for him for nerves.*

**10am-12pm:** *Leroy is sleeping a lot due to pain medications. Headache is a 6. He is getting another stole softener called Cena.*

**12pm:** *Neurocritical Care Physician visit/update: Leroy looks good. He is moving ahead of schedule. He really needs to have a bowel movement. The narcotics are causing constipation. With Leroy not eating enough food, they are keeping an eye on the bowels as it relates to the colon. Leroy is way ahead of healing for someone who has this level of blood on the brain.*

**12:18pm:** *His temperature is 98.5. Sitting in the chair since 9am. He does much better sitting up so it seems. Gravity is able to drain more fluid off the brain in this position. Due to his physical strength, he is able to minimize being bedridden.*

**1pm:** *He had a surge with the headache. We do not know the level. The speech-language pathologist is working with Leroy with swallowing and eating.*

**2pm:** *We are not sure what's going on with Leroy at this time. The headache is at an 8 out of 10 again. He has been sleeping all day off and on. He is spacey, rocking from side to side, confused about where he is, cold/wrapped in four blankets. He has struggled with swallowing. He appears to have phlegm in his throat or maybe not swallowing/chewing because he is really groggy.*

**3pm-3:30pm:** *The nurse kept reporting Leroy's look and strange things that he was witnessing. It was apparent that no one was taking the nurse nor my observations seriously. "Look at Leroy. He says he's in Arkansas. A minute later he's at his brother's house. He did not know where he was. It's not normal," the nurse kept saying.*

*I just stomped my foot at the doctor on duty and insisted that you do not give me text book stuff. "Look at Leroy. See what he does. He says he's in Arkansas. A minute later he's at his brother's house. He did not know where he was. It's not normal. He was staring into space," I insisted.*

*The doctor on duty is ordering an EEG to ensure Leroy is not having a seizure.*

**3:45pm-5pm:** *Leroy slept off and on.*

**5:15pm.** *He was served dinner. He ate a small amount of food.*

**5:45pm-7pm:** *Leroy slept off and on until I left. Nurses were administering pain medication for the constant headache.*

## Friday, August 6, 2021: Family That Prays Together Stays Together

*After yesterday's episode, they are checking to see if Leroy may have had a seizure. Doing an EEG in 5 minutes. Need prayer now for a "negative report."*

**8:17am:** *I sent out a prayer request. PRAYER REQUEST NOW PLEASE!*

*Leroy needs a bowel movement. It has been seven days. They are really pushing him to have one. They did an X-ray of his colon yesterday and said it was good. Pray for a bowel movement today in the name of Jesus. Amen*

**3:05pm: <u>Answered Prayer</u>:** *Leroy had two bowel movements.*

*In many ways, Leroy is improving beyond the doctor's expectations! Thank you so much for the continued prayers. They are needed and appreciated for and by him and our family! We see God's hand in so many ways. The testimony will be powerful!!!*

**4:46pm:** *Hey Everybody: Leroy is headed down to do a MRI & MRI-A. Pray for positive reports. I prayed with him and his nurse. By the way, he had 2 bowel movements. His headache has been between 0-3. Keep pouring on the prayers. I even got to take a nap up here today.*

*Neurocritical Care Physician Latest Update: He thinks Leroy had multiple strokes in the cerebellum because of the surgeries. What* this really means: this could affect his coordination. He feels that since he has made a lot of progress with everything this may not affect him. EEG was normal. At this point, the enemy cannot do us any more harm than God allows. I bind up the negative report from Neurocritical Care Physician in the name of Jesus. I loose in the name of Jesus that Leroy will make a 100% recovery in every area. In Jesus name I pray. Amen.

## Saturday, August 7, 2021: Moving Forward

*8:45am:* Leroy was awake, talking especially now that Shelton, his oldest son, is here to stay all day. He took his medications. His headache level stayed mostly at a zero; however, occasionally rising to a level 3 off and on.

He was extremely talkative and awake a lot. They have started to wean him from the narcotics such as morphine, hydrocodone, etc. He is now getting Tylenol 500mg to manage his headache pain. He ate really well.

## Week Two in NCCU
## Sunday, August 8, 2021: A Friend Who Sticks Closer Than A Brother

*All day, Leroy rested. He slept, ate and just had a peaceful day.*

## Monday, August 9, 2021: Faith Without Works Is Dead

*8.9.21 UPDATE ON LEROY:* He slept from **3:30pm-5:45pm**. He talked and sang all day. He walked to the bathroom and used the real toilet instead of urinal. No headache. He is off a lot of medicines. He is really good. Praise the Lord.

## Tuesday, August 10, 2021: The Right Word, The Right Time, The Right Way

*8:30am:* MRI/MRI-Down to finish the MRI because he could not complete—Leroy experienced claustrophobia.

***9:50am:*** *His speech is so much clearer for the complete sentences! WOW!!!!! WOW!!!!! I am praising God!!!*

***10am-10:25am:*** *Reading Leroy's devotional to him and praying over him. Leroy started praying out loud quoting scriptures so loud and clear. So like God—abundantly above and beyond! Bro. Nick is with him now.*

***11:25am:*** *NNeurocritical Care Physician just reported on the MRI. It showed a stroke in the cerebellum which is common. It has not and will not stop his progress for healing. It is not serious. On yesterday I received a call from one of our close friends after he saw the Instagram post from Princess. Our friend played professional football for 10 years and he had a stroke in the cerebellum last year. He was in the hospital for only 3 days. He found out because he had a bad headache that would not go away. He had high blood pressure. He had to have speech therapy to regain his speech and it didn't hamper his walking at all. This is what I see with your dad. Speech is his major issue. For our friend, you would never know that anything happened to him. I needed someone who could identify with their personal experience. God provided this person. Praise the Lord!*

## **Wednesday, August 11, 2021: On The Movement**

***8.11.21 UPDATE:*** *It was a quiet day. He walked all the way down the hall and back with a harness and walker. The walking is strong with excellent strength in his legs considering he is mostly in the bed. He had his first real bowel movement. He balanced talking so much. The speech is really clear and strong when he slows down. This is a strategy from the speech therapist. The cerebellum part of the brain controls the tongue, mouth and throat muscles. This is why the speech sounds slurred and hard to understand. When the blood dissipates, the brain resets and these muscles will function the way they were designed. Keeping the muscles moving with the speech therapy is essential. His headache was a 4. He received Tylenol 500mg, which allows him to sleep more peacefully and less edgy. He slept for a long time. He was told about rehabilitation* *services. Your dad doesn't know that it is in-house meaning you stay at the facility for a prescribed timeframe. He had a good appetite including grapes, his favorite nuts and Gatorade. His attitude was upbeat, positive and less worried about his family, money, etc. A very good day.*

### Thursday, August 12, 2021: Raising Funds

***9:36am:*** *Leroy walking to the tune of "I Want You Around" by Arregola Sohn. 1-2-3-4 walk. 1-2-3-4 walk*

### Saturday, August 14, 2021:

*Leroy talked to his brother, Sam.*

*Princess, graduated Suma Cum Laude from the University of North Texas-Dallas with her bachelor's degree in Sports Marketing and communication. Although she graduated December 2020 online due to COVID-19, today's ceremony was for graduates to actually walk across the stage to receive their diploma. Leroy and I watched it online again. She walked across the stage to receive her college diploma today.*

*My mom visited Leroy after the graduation ceremony from 1:30 pm-7:00 pm.*

## Third Week in NCCU
## Sunday, August 15, 2021: To Everything a Season

*Ecclesiastes 3:1. "There is an occasion for everything, and a time for every activity under heaven." (NIV 2011)*

*Mrs. McClure's Classmate Asked—Is This Legit? A friend of our ours was responding to the text and emails. She responded: to my classmate: Yes, it is. This season is legitimate for the McClures. Leroy's recovery will impede upon his ability to work for the rest of this year and/or perhaps even longer. The McClures are self-employed. Mrs. McClure is with him in NCCU every day and isn't working either. She is worn out, but encouraged daily by his progress. Mr. McClure has a message on his FaceBook page thanking everyone for their support. Look at the GoFundMe page and see him and his son in the photo. In addition, we trust God for his healing and absolutely lay claim to God's promises. We see God's hand all over this by the mere fact that he is alive and thriving so quickly. Please continue to pray for your classmate who is a living testament of loving a man in sickness and in health. If you have any other questions, I would be more than happy to answer them.*

**A text to my sister on my dad's side:** *Hi Sis: I am still on my face and knees. My husband is still in the hospital. The Neurocritical Care Physician will be in tomorrow to look at the shunt in his head, which is draining fluid off the brain. Once this is out, we will know the level of headaches he might experience for about 3-4 weeks. Once he gets that out, they will observe him for 24 hours. When this gets the ok, he will be released to the in-house rehab place for 3-4 weeks. Then we have to get the schedule for radiation. It is my prayer that he is home by October 1. He really doesn't know that he will not work until next year. I hope to develop a prayer request list tonight. I have been tired, sleepy and now a migraine. There are so many things to do and decisions to make. No matter all that is coming against us, we are still trusting God!*

## Monday, August 16, 2021 What the Shunt You're Saying?

## Powerful Prayer

*"And Jesus answered and said unto it (the fig tree), No man eat fruit of thee hereafter FOREVER, And His disciples heard it.... And in the morning, as they passed by, they saw the fig tree dried up from the roots." (Mark 11:14, 20) READ, study and meditate. (Mark 11) Jesus is waking from Bethany to Jerusalem with His disciples. He's hungry, (verse 13). He sees a fig tree, it had leaves but it doesn't have fruit. Jesus knew it was a counterfeit, and it spoke to Jesus, saying no fruit here. Jesus, answered the tree and said unto it, "No man eat fruit of thee hereafter FOREVER, And his disciples heard it." Jesus cursed it at the root, and He answered it. Jesus answered the tree. Why? Because it spoke to Him first. (NIV 2011) The truth was, that the tree had no fruit, that tree was saying to Jesus. "Forget it, you are not getting anything to eat here." Just like the tree with no fruit, your circumstance speak to you. Are you standing against sickness? That sickness is speaking to you every day. Poverty will speak to you in the same way, if you allow it to, the biggest lie poverty says, "You can't afford it!" These situations are counterfeits. YOU, must SPEAK to them like Jesus spoke to the fig tree. Curse them at the root. Answer them with the Word. "By the stripes of Jesus Christ you were healed." Philippians 4:19 says, "My God meets ALL my needs according to His riches in glory by Christ Jesus." (NIV 2011) "I am more than a conqueror in Christ Jesus." "I overcome by the blood of the lamb And the Word of my testimony." "Great is the Peace of my children." (NIV 2011) YOU, SPEAKING WORDS OF FAITH, will change things for you. Jesus cursed the fig tree at the root...and it made a permanent change. Release your faith, the faith God gave you the moment you were born-again, and curse your stubborn circumstances and dry them up at the root. YOU, can get rid of them from the roots up. Delight to do God's "will" when you were born-again, God gave you the authority to live, to move, to reign over ALL things. It is God's "Will" TODAY, RIGHT NOW, REJOICE, to do His "Will". Say, "I will" AND*

GOD SAID, "Beloved, above ALL I pray you may prosper and be in good health just as your soul prospers." (your soul is your mind, your will and your emotions) "God has no greater joy than to hear that His children walk in truth." (3 John 1:2, 4; NIV 2011) Say, "I will." Love ♥ You_

**8.16.21 UPDATE:** Leroy had a tough night because he did not get much sleep. The TV stayed on all night. He watched more TV than usual. His headache level was between a 3-4. He at a big breakfast. He went to sleep after breakfast around 8am-9:45am. The physical therapists woke him up for his scheduled walk time. He exhibits more balance and control with extremely impressive strength. He is meticulous in taking the proper steps rather than rushing to walk. He needs very little assistance in walking.

Leroy's lunchtime (1pm) appetite was good where he ate the meat, some vegetables and fruit. Around 1:30pm, the speech therapist worked with him on various activities. With pain medicines (Tylenol 500mg), he slept from 1:45pm until 4pm.

**8.16.21 UPDATE:** Leroy had a tough night because he did not get much sleep. The TV stayed on all night. He watched more TV than usual. His headache level was between a 3-4.

In order to be discharged from the acute care of NCCU and move to the in-house rehabilitation facility, the thin tube goes out of the head into a chamber and bag called the external ventricular drain (EVD) must be removed. The doctors are cautiously optimistic that the EVD will come out this week and he will be off to rehab for 2-3 weeks. Around 10:30am, a visit from Neurocritical Care Physician had the following findings/conclusions: it was time to close the EVD drain and remove the shunt from his head. The first step is to close the drain for 24 hours, test the fluid for bacteria. The second step is to determine and manage his pain level. The third step is to remove the EVD. The neurologist has to remove the shunt (the tube). It is a step-by-step, and wait and see process. A pending request is in process to change the rehab facility to the Arlington location due to the heavy North Dallas traffic and a longer commute than the hospital he is now in. Today he had more naps because they were *managing his headache pain level of 3-4 with more pain medicines since the ventric drain clamp is closed. He is walking with the walker and no assistance from the PT therapist. He exhibits good balance and control with extremely impressive strength. He is meticulous in taking the proper steps rather than rushing to walk. Leroy's appetite increases every day. Because the tongue, mouth and throat muscles are controlled by the cerebellum part of the brain, he will need speech therapy. He is asked to slow down and articulate. He is working hard at this.*

*Overall his progress is far ahead of schedule for all that he was faced with on his arrival to the NCCU on Friday, July 30, 2021 and then a vessel that burst along with two surgeries.*

CHAPTER 3

# Different Strokes for Different Folks

Stroke can happen to anyone at any time. Stroke is a "brain attack". Stroke recovery is a lifelong process. Stroke is the 5th leading cause of death in the U.S. There are nearly 7 million stroke survivors in the U.S. (About Stroke 2022)

From what I have learned about strokes, it impairs people in different ways, some physically and others cognitively or both. I was impaired physically and my sister-in-law was impaired cognitively losing 5% of her short-term memory. After many weeks of conversations and prayers, Monica and her husband decided she would come to Texas and go to CNS and get therapy with me. She left her home in Arkansas to live with us for five months. The two of us were picked up at 7:30 am Monday through Friday by CNS van for therapy sessions from 9:00 am to 2:00 pm. We ate lunch together every day and I saw much healing while she was with us at CNS. She was a joy to hang out with and it was a joy to introduce her to my friends. Daily we had good conversations and laughter. We not only experienced life but we experienced life more abundantly.

Despite all we have been through with our stroke, we recognize how we are now better and not bitter. When she came around Thanksgiving, I was out of the wheelchair. Even though she never saw me in the wheelchair, she saw me barely walking trying to get around. She was always there to help me when I was just experiencing life. When she was around me, I was like a whole person.

One day I wore a Fedora hat to therapy. It was a very windy day. The van pulled up at CNS and we got out of the van. I was the last one to get out since I moved the slowest. She waited patiently for me outside the van. The minute I stood up outside the van, the wind blew my hat off my head. I didn't move, I just watched it happen. She immediately took a couple steps, caught up with the hat and snatched it out of the air. I have never in my life seen her move so quickly and precisely. She had snagged the hat before I recognized it was missing from my head. I was thinking to myself goodbye hat because I can't chase you down but my sister-in-law always made me feel more complete when she was in my presence.

I could be squeezing a ball with my left hand working on my fine motor skills, then I would drop the ball. Since Monica knew how painful and difficult it was for me to retrieve the ball, she would have it in her hand ready to give it to me about the same time I was ready to get up and retrieve it myself. Again, her stroke didn't affect her physically. Now it looked like Monica was now well. Looks can be deceiving. Our family had to learn that a stroke manifest itself differently in each person. Let's not jump to conclusion that a stroke patient is now healed because they look normal.

## A King's Heart - My Son with HCM

Today, my family and I have experienced both heart disease and stroke. Usually it is common for a person to have had a stroke, and a heart attack because some of the same risk factors are involved with both. For example, diabetes, high blood pressure, and stress can contribute to a stroke and a heart attack. Like me, with my stroke, I had no symptoms; now my son was diagnosed with a heart condition and he had no symptoms. At the age of 18, our son, King, was diagnosed with HCM during his freshman year in 2015 at Baylor University.

## Beating the Odds

It was June of 2015 when I received a phone call from Baylor University Athletic Trainer sharing with me that my son had a heart problem and further testing was needed. I was devastated. I cannot explain to you what all was going through my mind. My son had just graduated from high school two weeks before and he was now in college on a basketball scholarship. After I gained my composure and became rational, I asked how was King's attitude about this unfortunate situation? The trainer said his attitude was good until King was told he couldn't practice nor dribble a basketball until further testing. Over the next several weeks, we traveled across the country getting tested by the best cardiologists from Seattle Washington to Rochester, Minnesota and it was finally revealed that King had HCM - Hypertrophic Cardiomyopathy, an enlarged heart. All of us were aware of basketball players dying on the basketball court from this disease. Most of the doctors were telling King he needed to quit playing basketball. This 18-year-old young man loved the game of basketball and he wasn't going to listen to such negative advice from the doctors across the country.

Finally, King received some positive news. He received a phone call from former Phoenix Suns Head Basketball Coach and now the Detroit Pistons Head Coach. He told King he has HCM also and he not only played basketball in college for Notre Dame but he also played in the NBA for 15 years. He told King God is still in control, not the doctors and he will get to play basketball again. Meanwhile, Baylor's Head Basketball Coach was not only praying with us on a regular basis, but he was searching across the world for doctors believing in athletes with HCM can still play sports. Before he contacted them, he made it crystal clear to King and us that Baylor 4-year scholarship to King was still good even if he chose to not play basketball anymore. King told his coach that he wants to play basketball if he can.

His coach kept searching and finally he set up a meeting with the Mayo Clinic in Minnesota. We met with the Head Cardiologist after he did a few tests on King. The Head Cardiologist asked King what was his main goal. King said his goal was to play basketball for the Baylor Bears. He responded to King saying I believe we can make that happen. The cardiologist proceeded to explain what must take place like implanting a defibrillator into King's stomach which will be monitored for 24-hours. After hearing all of this, I wasn't sure if I wanted him to still play the game but King was sure. There was no doubt in his mind. I thought to myself, King is braver than I am. This young man is not needing this heart surgery to stay alive but just to play basketball. At the conclusion of the meeting, The Head Cardiologist asked to finish the day with prayer. He asked me to dial up and he would hang up. It was at this time when I decided my family would be better and not bitter from this life changing event.

On October 1, 2017, King's 19th birthday, he was cleared to play basketball for the Baylor University Bears basketball team. King worked harder than he has ever worked to get back in shape to play the game at college level. He did not miss a beat. He played in Baylor's opening game after being told he wouldn't play basketball again. God had the final say on King's basketball career. He went on to play for Baylor University for four years without any heart issues. I started second guessing God. Why my son? He's a good young man. This enlarged heart is keeping him from having a chance to play professional basketball in the NBA. We have spent his entire life preparing him for the NBA, then this heart situation happens without warning. After all of this stinking thinking, I decided I would not allow Satan to get a toehold, foothold nor a stronghold. I recognized that Satan comes to kill, steal and destroy, but Jesus says He came so we may have life and have life more abundantly. (John 10:10) (NIV 2011) With this in mind, I decided to not become bitter, I became better to use King's story to give God the glory. King is now the youngest ESPN Basketball Analyst and spokesman for American Heart and Stroke Association. He's on television and speaking around the country all the time.

It was six years later before I came close to death by having a stroke in the gym to understand the fight and through my son's determination to play basketball again. His story propelled me to work hard, keep my healing goals before me and make the most of the stroke's journey.

For family and friends, I started a Facebook post so that everyone could follow my journey of recovery in real time.

## The Facts About a Stroke

The center of your body is controlled by the brain. It controls how you think, feel, communicate, and move. Knowing how your brain works, can help you understand your stroke. The brain is full of specialized cells called neurons. These neurons make the brain work. To work properly – and even to survive – they need to be fed by constant supply of blood. The brain is made up of arteries and veins. Arteries carry blood, rich in oxygen and nutrients to your organs. Veins carry waste products away from your organs.

The brain is divided into six regions, called the hemisphere. The regions include four lobes, frontal lobe, parietal lobe, temporal lobe, cerebellum, and brain stem. Each of these areas controls different functions in the body.

My hemorrhagic stroke occurred in the AVM, which is located in the cerebellum, which controls, balance, motor, movement, coordination, posture, and fine motor skills. For me, the weakness and balance problems puts me at risk of falling.

My sister-in-law's ischemic stroke was caused by the blood clotting as it relates to having AFib, Arterial fibulation, which is a type of irregular heart rhythm. Her stroke related issue was with the occipital lobe, which covers vision, interpreting what you see. Also, she had some damage to about 5% of the part of the brain that stores short term memory, which is the ability to hear something immediately and remember how to do it.

When the blood stops flowing to any part of your brain, it can cause a stroke or even death if not treated quickly. This interruption causes damage to the brain cells which cannot be repaired or replaced. The effects of your strokes depend on the part of the brain that was damaged and the amount of damage done.

The effects of a stroke are time sensitive. The first hours of a stroke are very critical. The healthcare providers will be working quickly to figure out the type of stroke, how they can make the right diagnoses through a CT scan, to stabilize a person, to provide early treatment.

Think **F.A.S.T.** when you see the signs of a stroke. (About Stroke 2023) Here are the recommendations from National Center for Chronic Disease Prevention and Health Promotion (NCCDPHP).

**F** = Face Drooping – Does one side of the face droop or is it numb? Ask the person to smile. Is the person's smile uneven?

**A** = Arm Weakness – Is one arm weak or numb? Ask the person to raise both arms. Does one arm drift downward?

Watch for sudden:

**S** = Speech Difficulty – Is speech slurred?

**T** = Time to Call 911 – Stroke is an emergency.

## Professional Healthcare Team

Treatment and recovery time occurs at different times for different people. Recovery starts once you are stabilized. For a stroke victim, a comprehensive care consists of the following types of doctors, specialties and experts as follows: Occupational therapist, PT, speech-language, pathologist, case manager, and dietitian helps you to know the treatment.

## Recovery vs Rehabilitation

Recovery start as soon as a person is ready. Rehabilitation is a long-term process and approach that helps you to recover as many abilities as possible. It can be a formal program or one that you may do on your own at home. Recovery is a long-term process – the length of time varies from one person to the next. For some people, recovery can take several months and for others progress can continue to happen over a long period of time.

It is important to know, that, in the first two weeks after a stroke, some of the abilities may start to return as your brain, naturally recovers, such as swallowing, speaking, understand what people are saying, or moving affected arm or leg. Which is also very important. The brain is able to make up for functions lost in damaged areas. It reorganizes and re-wires itself. Disability is called Neuro plasticity. The goal of stroke rehabilitation is to help a person recover as much function as possible. (About Stroke 2023)

To make changes in the brain, you need to train it by repeating specific exercises and activities. The type of rehab you do depends on it, if the very stroke is common to the part of brain that was affected. The effects of stroke on your body, mind and emotions, and your general health, depends of a person's ability to actively take part in their recovery, and the support system of family caregivers. Whatever you put into your recovery, you get something out of it. And just remember nothing from nothing leaves nothing.

## The Angiogram Defined/Further Explained

**What is an Angiogram?** This is the most detailed test to diagnose an AVM.

The angiogram test reveals the location and characteristics of the feeding arteries and draining veins, which is critical to planning treatment.

## The Angiogram Results

According to the Interventional Neuroradiology Physician, the Angiogram was successful for me. They went in to explore which one of the three vessels that lead to the AVM part in the cerebellum of the brain ruptured and needed the blood flow stopped permanently. They located the vessel that ruptured on Friday which also re-ruptured on Sunday.

The Interventional Neuroradiology Physician came in and talked to Jenna and me. He revealed to us that they found the vessel, which was the same one on Friday (while working out at the gym) and Sunday (11:30am while waiting to have the Angiogram). They embolized the vessel using a glue-like substance called Onyx, which is designed to permanently seal it and prevent any more bleeding.

The doctors performed part one of a two-part effective treatment for people with AVM.

**Part 1 Treatment: Endovascular embolization.** The doctors performed this on Sunday, August 1, 2021. In this procedure, the doctor inserts a long, thin tube (catheter) into leg artery and threads it through blood vessels to your brain using X-ray imaging. The catheter is positioned in one of the feeding arteries to the AVM, and injected Onyx, an embolization agent, such as small particles, a glue-like substance to block the artery and reduce blood flow into the AVM.

Endovascular embolization is less invasive than traditional surgery. The Interventional Neuroradiology Physician said that the embolization is used prior to other surgical treatments or radiation to make the procedure safer by reducing the size of the AVM or the likelihood of bleeding again.

**The new issue:** The doctors and I have to determine how to prevent actual AVM in the brain so to prevent a rupture, which will cause a major stroke. There are two options that we must decide on within 90 days. They are explained as Part 2/Option 1 and Option 2.

**Part 2/Option 1: Stereotactic radiosurgery (SRS).** This treatment uses precisely focused radiation to destroy the AVM. It is not surgery in the literal sense because there is no incision. Instead, SRS directs many highly targeted radiation beams at the AVM to damage the blood vessels and cause scarring. The scarred AVM blood vessels then slowly clot off in one to three years following treatment. This treatment is most appropriate for small AVMs that are difficult to remove with conventional surgery and for those that haven't caused a life-threatening hemorrhage.

**Part 2/Option 2:** Microsurgery is a term for the surgical resection of an AVM. This is a common treatment option for AVMs that are surgically accessible and often provides a complete cure. The doctors will determine if the AVM is surgically accessible.

The healing has been done. Going forward, Leroy will need to have a PT, OT, and speech therapist. In order to regain his walking, talking and physical mobility, the three types of therapy need to start immediately.

The doctor said it will take 3 to 4 months for Leroy to fully recover from the embolization of those tangled vessels. Then we need to consider which option to go to. Leroy will be in the hospital for the rest of this week. The PT, OT & speech therapists will start to work with him.

For family and friends, Leroy started Facebook post so that everyone followed his journey of recovery in real time. In Chapter 6, you will see post on various situations that he informed family and friends about.

CHAPTER 4

# Loving. Healthy. Recovery.

Stroke affects everyone differently and rehabilitation helps with the effects of stroke. Rehabilitation is where you work on things that have changed since your stroke. The two facilities and its rehabilitation and therapy approaches are discussed as follow:

> **SCHEDULE**
>
> - Three hours of therapy, five days per week
> - 24/7 nursing care, including nurses who specialize in rehabilitation
> - Frequent visits from a physician

**Arlington Encompass Hospital**

I was excited about being transported to Encompass in Arlington Texas for many reasons. First, I recognized I was going to live and I saw the outside for the first time in three weeks. This was a ten-mile bumpy trip in the evening approaching darkness. I recognized the ride was very bumpy because my pain level increased with each bump. Finally, we made it to the rehab hospital. Two men rolled me in to Arlington Encompass Hospital to my private room. Despite my room having two beds, my bed was the only one being occupied. I was experiencing headaches and I was medicated so heavily that all I wanted to do was sleep. I slept like anew born baby the first night in my new room.

Rehab started the next morning. An Occupational Therapist was in my room to help me get to the toilet and to help me take a shower. I first had to learn how to stand up, then transfer to my wheelchair. I was pushed in the wheelchair into the bathroom then I had to stand up again, transfer to the toilet. The caregiver would give me privacy until I was done. I would call her in to help me transfer to the wheelchair. Then, she would push me toward the shower and I would make the transfer to the shower wheelchair. After a week or two, I learned how to use the toilet and take a shower all by myself. Transferring to and from the wheelchair took 2-3 weeks for me to master. I was in good physical condition prior to my stroke, but my legs had to get stronger: therefore, I was not allowed to make the transfer from the wheelchair by myself. This was just good safety protocol. I didn't realize until later that I had to do all of this every morning before my therapy sessions started.

## Encompass Therapy

If the truth be told, I was already worn out before therapy started. I kept telling God there must be another way. I would eat breakfast at 7:30 am then therapy would start at 8:30 am. This lady we called Sarg would get us started or warmed up in a group session. Initially, I thought she was mean, but I recognized she was just what I needed. She acted just like a sergeant. If you were late or tried to sleep in, she would come and get you out of the bed and help you get ready so you could make it to her class even with a headache. She would call your nurse and your nurse would come to her class, check your vital signs, give you medicine and then leave you there with Sarg.

The exercises we did in group sessions weren't all that. But after coming from a stroke or out of brain surgery, those exercises were just what I needed. We did exercises for about 45-50 minutes. After 2 weeks, I got good at this. In fact, when Sarg needed to go and get someone out the bed, she let me lead the group until she came back. As a natural born leader, it's hard to not get noticed whether you are sick or healthy. After the session, Sarg would push me in a wheelchair back to my room until my next therapy session. I usually would have 30 minutes to 1 hour to rest. My wife would visit me during this time and she would stay until closing (7:00 pm) every day for 21 days.

I kept getting stronger with the help of my Physical Therapist, Occupational Therapist and Speech Therapist. Every day I worked out with them and my goal for each one of them was to be the best patient I could be. Unfortunately, the therapists were off on weekends, Saturday and Sunday. My wife would get there around 10 am on Saturday. Some days she would push me outside to get some sunlight, but she was late one day so I decided to have a pity party for myself until I met this nurse. This strong-willed Black woman came in my room and blessed me out after listening to her colorful words, I decided to get my act together or else she was going to body slam my helpless body. She told me to get my funky body up and take a shower. I was still waiting for my wife to get there. This day was a lonely day for me. I had planned to stay in bed all day and not take a shower until I saw Yvette. Apparently, I was spoiled. Once I saw my wife, I was good and the nurse had already told her about my behavior. After a few minutes, my wife and I laughed about the whole ordeal.

## Get Up & Walk Again

If I was going to learn how to walk again, my work ethic was not going to be a problem. In fact, I was willing to do more than the expectations of the therapists. I believed God was in control, and I talked and prayed with him without ceasing. I knew that Faith without work is dead. Despite me getting stronger and being able to stand from the time I had been at Encompass, I still was not able to walk. I continued to work hard at exercise and doing everything my therapists asked me to do with a positive attitude. There were many nurses and caretakers working with me. Some days were very difficult for me because I did not like all of these people seeing me naked. One reason I was concerned was because I hadn't been home in 40+ days and it appeared everyone was seeing me naked except my wife.

Even though I was there to get well, this wasn't fair. My wife thought this was hilarious until I told her about this lady flirting with me. My stroke affected me physically, not cognitively. My body was in constant pain along with occasional headaches. I praise God for my wife being there to see me every day and many times my daughters, Princess and Jenna would come to see me and pray with me also. There were times when I was down or even bitter but these women kept giving me hope to get better and live on. I found so much comfort in encouraging other patients to have hope and I continued to get better. I knew I would eventually walk but I didn't know how it would be initiated. I was not worrying about walking at all. I knew since I was doing all of the prerequisites, it was just a matter of time.

One day my wife was there visiting me and I told her if she gave me some, I would start walking. She laughed but I told her I was serious. So I gave her the sad story about me not being home in almost 40 days and everybody is seeing me naked except her. That's not fair and if she gives me some, I would walk. I told her I was very serious, I really believed that. She said, "Okay Lee, let's do it." I told her to lock the door and she did that. I didn't know what to do next. I figured out quickly after having a stroke and brain surgery, things didn't work the same. Once she said we don't have all day, I had to figure out something in a hurry. I was surprisingly limited with my mobility of what all I could do. At the end of the day, praise God, I was successful. I've been married for over 25 years, but man, this time it was different, I mean really different. I believe I developed a new pathway in my brain. The next day I was transferring from the wheelchair to the bed and Yvette was about 10 feet away from me. As I got out of the wheelchair, I stood straight up and Yvette said, "Lee, walk to me." I walked to her without any hesitation. Once I got to her, I didn't know what to do so she put her arms around me and hugged me. This kept me from falling. Then she gently laid me down in the bed. I must have said, "Baby, I just walked," at least 8 times. That night and the night before was the best sleep I had received at this rehab facility. No, I was not ashamed of my behavior for those two days. In fact, I was thinking about doing it again but it was a whole lot of work and I ran out of time. When I was initially scheduled to leave the rehab, I had many employees wanting to come by and say goodbye to me. Some of them had purchased one of my books and wanted me to autograph it. Others were spreading the rumor that I was a celebrity and I was about to be discharged. It was all good and an expression of their love.

## My Cousin Cle

The day was Sunday, September 12, 2021, my wife's birthday. My Cousin Cle Jones brought me some barbecue ribs to the rehab facility. He sneaked the ribs into my room. He was late getting the ribs to me, but it was worth the wait. My cousin was one of the most reliable people I know. We grew up together in Conway, Arkansas. When I had my stroke on July 30, 2021, he was one of the first ones to be there at the hospital while I was waiting for my wife to get there from being out of town. This day was special because he knew I enjoyed barbecue ribs and it had been more than six weeks since I had real food. In the summer, we ate our share of barbecue ribs. I waited and waited for him to bring me the ribs, but he brought me more than the ribs. He brought his mom and sister from Arkansas over to visit me, what a surprise! The ribs were no longer important after seeing Cousin Mary and Cousin Jeanie. It was a very emotional time; I couldn't control my tears. Cousin Mary and my mother were best friends. Cousin Mary was a mother figure to me and I had just lost my mother in February 2021. Cousin Mary was excited to see me first hand and realized despite me being in a wheelchair, I was going to be alright. Then Cle brought the barbecue ribs in. We had a good time during the visit of my cousins and those ribs were good too. I still can't figure out how Cle was able to get these visitors to come in at the same time to visit me when we were only allowed one visitor at a time. Toward the end of our gathering, Cle brought his lovely wife in and prayed with me.

It's this type of moments that gives you hope and drives you to keep living so you can do the same for someone else. What a special day and birthday my wife had, it was worth all the waiting.

## Good Bye Encompass

My insurance coverage would not allow me to stay much longer after 21 days at Encompass. I wasn't walking. I was not ready to go home and be a burden to my wife. I am trusting God to work something out. The CEO of Encompass recognized our challenge; therefore, he recommended The Centre for Neuro Skills (CNS), a more advanced rehab in Irving, Texas. We were still looking at inpatient care since I was not ready to go home. My wife and daughter went to visit CNS and they loved it. If I agree, I would live in CNS patient apartment with a roommate, a nurse would oversee my medical care, a 24-hour nurse in the apartments, a CNS driver to take a patient to the clinic for rehabilitation. For this dream to come true, my wife had to change insurance coverage. It happened just in time. To make this happen, we had to get new insurance coverage. On September 13, 2021, I was transferred to the Centre for Neuro Skills for impatient rehabilitation. The ambulance ride to CNS was challenging but I managed it. It was my first day being outside the rehab facility in three weeks.

## Centre for Neuro Skills - Life Saver

In order for me to be successful at CNS, I had to succeed in three areas: apartment living, therapy at the clinic and carpool by van when I started outpatient services. I had to understand the ABC's of life saving therapy.

## Apartment Living

It had been almost 30 years since I had lived in an apartment: therefore, I had to make a major transition. After two weeks, I made that adjustment to living in the apartments. Unfortunately, my family couldn't visit me every day because of the COVID-19 outbreak. The rules were very simple for the family. They could only visit me during the weekend. Initially, I had a problem with that rule, however, we learned how to comply. There were other rules I had to adjust to but most of them were designed for us to learn how to live independently and to practice safety protocol as we rehab.

The nurses made sure we took our medicine at the appropriate time. The apartment living was designed for us to become more independent while we were receiving therapy at the clinic. Caretakers made certain you could move around in your apartment from the kitchen to the toilet, shower or bedroom. We had a caretaker with us 24 hours at all time when we were not receiving therapy. They had supervisors coming to the apartments to observe them throughout the day. Sometimes they walk into our apartment without knocking. We have to lock the doors to keep this from happening.

Once a supervisor walked into our place with an attitude and started asking too many questions without introducing herself. I don't roll like that so I had to put her in her place. My response went like this. "Who do you think you are to come in my home without knocking nor introducing yourself and then asking us 100 questions? This is total disrespect; therefore, any questions you may ask the answer is none of your damn business. Let's have a do over. Now once you go out the door and knock, then we will answer the door. We will invite you in, then you can tell us who you are and what is the reason of your the visit. Not only did we get respect after the do over but we used this as a teaching moment for new supervisors. Treat people the way you would like to be treated. I've figured it out, just because we are in a wheelchair, my roommate and I will not be disrespected or taken advantage of. Maybe, this is how you do it at other apartments, but not here. We demand respect or we will go to the top and file a complaint. Because of my leadership experience, I know what it takes to get positive results. Let's remember the stroke impaired me physically not cognitively. My mind is still that of a CEO. I'm observing everything that's going on around me and I'm taking mental notes as I become stronger.

## CNS Therapy

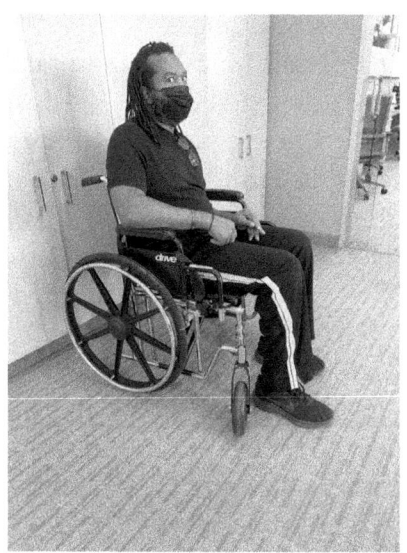

*Figure 2 Roll On! Getting to roll myself to class*

For me to be successful at CNS, I had to understand the ABC's of life saving therapy. CNS is the bridge to meaningful life. Satan comes to kill steal and destroy. Jesus says He came so we may have life and have life more abundantly. (John 10:10) (NIV 2011) My goal was not just to live but also to thrive while living. I wanted to see my life transformed so I can help other patients have abundant life. It started with my attitude. Yes, I was mad at God for a moment, not a minute, not an hour, not a day but for a short moment. And I recognized my attitude was negative. I recognized it stunk. The devil is a liar, he comes to kill, steal and destroy. He tried his best to get a strong hold of my attitude but I wouldn't let him. Then he tried to get a foothold and I wouldn't let him. Then he tried again to get a toehold, but I had to rebuke him in the name of Jesus. As a mature Christian, I had to get my mind right. My Bible tells me our Lord never makes a mistake; therefore, I needed to stop thinking woe is me and be grateful I'm still alive. I needed to humble myself and exalt the Lord, and He would take it from there and it started with my attitude.

ATTITUDE determines your altitude. Nothing positive happens unless you have a positive attitude. In fact, no one wants to be around negative people. Negative people are everywhere, there is no shortage of negative people. I call them joy busters. They try to steal your joy. My attitude was very simple. I told everyone I worked with, my goal was to be the best patient I could be. I was going to be a good soldier. Whatever I did, I did it as if I was doing it for the

Lord and not for man. I am a soldier in the army of the Lord. Despite being poorly sick, all I wanted was my medicine and to sleep, I knew the Lord would make a way if I had the right attitude.

BELIEVE in Christ. Believe in yourself, your therapists, and counselor. Even when you don't understand what they were doing or saying, just do it and believe them. They are the professionals. Just like the heavens are so much higher than the earth, so are God's ways so much higher than our ways and so are His thoughts much higher than our thoughts. (Isaiah 55:8-9) (NIV 2011) Let's face the truth, we don't know everything. We have finite minds. Despite some of us being leaders, we are sick and we must learn to follow.

CARRY your own load. You can't just show up at CNS every day and think you will get better. You must put in the work. The work is not easy but it's worth the effort. There is no substitute for hard work. Laziness pays off now but hard work pays off for the future. Do the work with enthusiasm when you could.

Getting therapy at CNS was one of the best thing that happened to me. It was a life saver. I'm talking about education therapy, cognitive therapy, occupational therapy and physical therapy. I was put on the walking program during my second week. Despite being in the wheelchair, they recognized the progress that Encompass had made with me while I was there for 21 days. One of the Physical Therapists (PT), a petite woman, told me I could walk and all I needed to do was stand up from my wheelchair, take her hand and she would show me I can walk. Behind her was a muscle bound man I thought to be a bodyguard. I stood up, took her hand and we walked together. That muscular man was not a bodyguard, he was there to guard my body in case of a fall. He followed right behind me as I was walking side by side with the PT as I was holding her hand. The PT Department went to work on me immediately.

With three weeks of therapy, I was out of the wheelchair using my walker. It wasn't easy, I was huffing and puffing along the way. Some nights while in bed, my entire body was killing me. I would cry, pray and do a few stretches to ease the pain. At one time it was so painful and difficult to walk that I once said walking was overrated. I wanted to quit and become bitter but I knew God had a bigger plan for me. It wasn't all about me. Since I'm here, how can I be a blessing to others? I always have been a leader, not a quitter. How can I help others if I am a quitter? After spending some time with the Lord, I decided to work on my attitude.

I also was blessed with an understanding counselor at CNS. He is very smart and wise. As a strong-willed Black man that has been in leadership positions for over 25 years, I felt I didn't need a counselor. In my neighborhood, having a counselor, psychiatrist or psychologist was a sign of weakness. I initially thought CNS was losing its mind by putting me with a counselor without my consent. After having a stroke, the first thing I had to accept was I didn't know it all, now. My wife is right 100% of the time and CNS knows more about my brain than I do.

*Figure 3 Long Way to Home: At home practicing walking with a walker*

My counselor was the best. I talked and he listened not just with his ears but also with his heart. His feedback was not only on point but he was a blessing to me and my family. My counselor is blessed with heavenly wisdom and he is an asset to CNS. I thank God for him daily. When other patients would ask me how I am doing, I would tell them I'm doing 100. This meant 100%. Weekly, my 100 kept increasing; therefore, other patients took my lead and tried to keep up with me. Patients were using my numbering system to display their feelings when being asked. Some would respond by saying, I'm not doing as good as Leroy, but I'm doing .......

I implemented this numbering system to increase self-esteem, show progress and build up positive attitudes. Great things happen in a positive environment. If you are around me enough, you will see this being played out. If not, maybe you are too negative and if I can't change that attitude with my personality or prayers, I must leave you behind. There are too many people at CNS that needs healing not a pity party. There was so much therapy and love in this place that I was not in a hurry to leave.

On the outside, people tend to treat you according to what you have or don't have. I saw this first hand as a CEO for 20 years. I saw the good and bad of many people according to my position. I thank God I had a relationship with Him because I was in prayer for most of these people and my heart was always purified with the obedience of the truth. I always treated people like I wanted to be treated. This is why I loved being at CNS and we all are moving on up at our own speed. They don't blatantly talk about Jesus at CNS but I can tell the power of the Holy Spirit was there and being activated. I know this to be true because I'm a living proof.

## Carpool

After having therapy and being an in-patient at CNS for six weeks, it was time for me to live at home and be transported to CNS for rehabilitation. Physically, I had made progress and I was able to get out of the wheelchair and walk. CNS agreed to transport me from home to the clinic and back home when therapy was over for the day five days a week. At that time, it was difficult for me to ride in an automobile after having surgery on my brain and I was having headaches to all bumps while riding in a vehicle.

I could not ride in the car with just anybody. Riding with a driver was frightening for me after just getting out of the wheelchair. It appeared the car was always moving too fast for me and the car ran over every pothole and bump in the streets. The first few weeks of riding with a driver was not good, however, I learned to make the adjustments. Initially, I was only comfortable riding in a wheelchair, slow but steady. I eventually learned that 35mph in a car wasn't too fast. It didn't take me long to figure that the best place for me was to ride in the back seat.

It took my driver over one hour to drive me to the clinic and one hour to take me home. I had to make this carpool work because my wife was not able to take me to rehab every day. Yvette and I started praying about my carpool situation. The CNS carpool was an ideal situation for us. Therefore, I needed to get with the program and make it work because the Lord had made provisions. Despite being uncomfortable riding in a car and having headaches when the car ran over potholes and bumps, I needed to make this work or else I could possibly miss out on receiving the best therapy from CNS after having a stroke.

## CHAPTER 5

# Leroy's Walking Club

**Walking - One Million Steps Later**

For me, I describe the process of walking as a 5-step process.

1. wheelchair
2. walker or cane
3. baby steps (5-10)
4. walking like a robot (many mini baby steps)
5. walk like a king (long steps)

I saw this young man way ahead of me walking like a robot. I called his name out and said let's race. I also told him I would give him a head start and we would walk to our next class. He agreed. I caught up with him, passed him and then I smoked him. I told all the male therapists about me kicking his butt. This man is a young man, 22 years old not wanting to put the work in that was necessary to improve his walking. In fact, he was waiting for his Botox shot then he said he would race me again and beat me: therefore, he didn't need to work on his walking. Everywhere he went, someone was teasing him about the old man out walking him. Prior to all of this, I tried to tell this young man not to go up and down the stairs unless someone was watching him. He needed to use the elevator like me and others. That young buck said he knows how to use the stairs and I said so do we, however, we choose to practice safety protocol. Now keep in mind he is at stage 4 in walking like a robot. Later on I saw one of his therapists and I asked her if it was okay for him to walk up and down the stairs without supervision. She seemed startled.

This day was also the same day that the young man had a conference with his parents and therapists. One of the therapists reported that the young man was seen going up and down the stairs without supervision. According to this young man, his parents went off on him and started screaming that he never listens with his hard head. I guess you are wondering how do I know all of this. This young man approached me and asked me if I was a snitch? I said yes. Then he went on to tell me he had a conference and what happened at the conference.

I told him what you do in the dark will always come to the light. He still tried to convince me that he knows how to go up and down the stairs. A man convinced against his own will is of the same opinion even still.

I reminded him how badly I beat him when we raced the other day. "It's obvious I'm more advanced in walking than you are, don't you agree?" He said yes. Despite me being faster than he is and I walked like a king and he walked like a robot, I chose to use the elevator every time because of safety protocol. CNS has been good to us and they have safety protocols in place for our own protection. Yes, I'm old school and yes I'm a snitch, but I always stand for what is right. Just because you can do something doesn't mean you need to do it if it goes against the company's policy. We need more people to stand up for what is right because it's the right thing to do.

Even at the age of 61, three months ago I had a conference with my wife, case worker, counselor and my therapists. We talked about my progress and I volunteered to tell them I walked up and down the stairs all by myself. I called myself boasting and thought it was a good thing. To my surprise, everybody jumped on me as if I had committed a crime. I took it like a grown man and agreed not to do that again. Since that time, I have used the stairs at least 10 times. Each time I made sure someone was watching me. I learned quickly that safety protocol is the only way. Therefore, I always use my personal experience to benefit other patients.

When I arrived at CNS apartments to live as an inpatient patient, I had no idea how my life would be transformed. I would take a nap at 2:30 p.m. Monday through Friday after finishing therapy sessions at CNS from 9am to 2pm. I was completely exhausted from the day mainly because of all the walking.

## Leroy's Walking Club

I had been at Centre for Neuro Skills (CNS) almost nine months and I was so grateful. CNS had been such a blessing to me that I really wanted to give back. I felt led to give back by creating a Leroy's Walking Club. I can't tell you how much positive public relations came from the walking club. Everyone was talking about it and many people wanted to join. I was getting requests from employees also. However, only patients could become members. After all, we were the ones learning how to walk again. I created Leroy's Walking Club t-shirts for those that joined Leroy's Walking Club. Our goal was to encourage and modeled what could happen after you got out of the wheelchair and started walking.

I started the walking club by walking daily inside the perimeter of CNS three to four times each day. I thought the best way to improve my walking was to strategically walk more. I set a personal goal of 1 million steps. I increased my walking from three to fifteen laps on the inside of CNS in three months as I built my endurance. One lap for me was approximately 550 steps and 15 laps was approximately 8,000 steps or 3.5 miles. I was taking 8,000 steps per day five times each week which was 40,000 steps each week or 160,000 steps each month. After seven months I passed 1,000,000 steps, equivalent to 437 miles. My motto was laziness pays off now but hard work pays off for the future. Faith without work is dead!

## Small Presentation

On Friday, May 13, 2022, I had an opportunity to do a presentation for about 25 people. Most of them were my new found friends, patients at CNS. My topic was on Changing the World. I did a PowerPoint on how I was changing the world before my stroke and how I will continue to change the word after the stroke. My wife and daughter were present along with a friend of the family. They all said I did a good job and I thank God for that. I felt very good doing the presentation. What excited me the most was my friends got to see the other side of me such as what I am passionate about and what really turns me on. Despite standing up for one hour during the presentation working on my endurance, I had a great time sharing with my friends how I keep hope alive even after a stroke.

## Meeting New Patients

My encounters with new patients at CNS were very therapeutic most days. I loved meeting new patients no matter what their health situation might have been. I take the initiative in meeting new patients because that's who I am even if they do not respond to me. I have three situations I would like to share with you that confirms my enjoyment with newcomers. After being at CNS for nine months, I met this brand new patient (new patient # 1) in the wheelchair and he didn't respond at all when I introduced myself to him. He was highly medicated for pain and he appeared to be asleep. Meeting someone new seemed like the last thing he wanted to do. I spoke to him several times each day. His lack of response was not going to change who I am. I went almost three weeks without seeing him. One day I was walking in the hallway and I heard someone calling my name from a distance.

I recognized the voice so I walked toward his wheelchair. It was my guy, the new patient of three weeks ago that wasn't responding to me. The man told me he had been sick and he missed me. He missed me because I showed him attention and love at one of his lowest moments. He could feel the joy I had within. Even today we enjoy a sweet fellowship. He is one of my closest friends at the clinic and even outside the clinic.

I met another new patient in a wheelchair and he had a helmet on. Initially, I was reluctant to go and meet him but the Holy Spirit told me to be bold and go meet him, and give him some love as an ambassador. I finally made my way over to him after trying to avoid him. He also was barely awake and after I told him my name, he repeated my name and said he was in pain. I asked him if he believed in prayer? He said yes and then I asked him if I could pray with him? He said yes again. I moved closer to him, grabbed his hand softly and whispered a prayer. I first thanked the Lord for my new friend and I asked Him if He would help us to remove the pain my friend was experiencing. I ended the prayer and then I opened my eyes and a therapist was there to take my new friend to the nurse office. My friend thanked me because he saw that prayer really works.

I have seen him several times since our initial visit and each time he makes it clear that he put a lot of trust in me. For example, as I walked my daily 8,000 steps, I passed by him and he asked if I could adjust his headrest for him. Keep in mind he has a high tech sophisticated wheelchair that's way out of my league. "I would love to help you but give me a minute," I told him. I went into the PT office and asked for assistance. They were eager to help. I continued my walk and I made it back to my friend to see if he was okay. He cheerfully thanked me for helping him. I went to the PT office again to thank them for helping my friend. Many time in life we must inspect what we expect and then show appreciation.

Lastly, this third patient I met was trying to figure me out. I introduced myself to him and he was very nice and alert. The next day he saw me in Physical Therapy and asked me if I would be working with him that day? I told him I was a patient just like him. Apparently, he didn't hear me or he didn't believe me because he asked me that question again. I responded this time by telling him I was in the wheelchair just like him for 10 weeks but now I'm walking. I am a patient just like you, but I will get a therapist to help you.

After seeing me talking to everyone for two days, I believe he saw me as someone in authority. Maybe he saw the pep in my step or heard the confidence in my voice. He was alert enough to know that something was different about me. Every day before I leave my house, I ask the Lord to order my steps and to empower me to be a blessing to all the people I may encounter. Some blessings come in the form of healing. I am a walking example of what God can do even after a stroke. I am now better not bitter. When you refresh others, you too will be refreshed.

## Annoying

There have been other times when my encounters with new patients at CNS were very awkward to say the least. Every day I go to therapy, I get to express my joy by speaking to someone. Unfortunately, we all were in rehab because of a stroke or a traumatic brain injury. When people asked me how I was doing, I had several positive ways to answer them. One way I answered them was by saying life is good, I'm on top of the earth instead of the earth on top of me. Despite all of our issues, we must still count our blessings. I loved to speak to all employees, patients and call them by their names. If I see them five different times, I would speak to them using their name each time.

For example, "What's up John? It's good to see you again John" or "Hello John. How is your day going?" Since I have four classes every day, I literally would speak to some people four to five times a day. Repeating their names helped me memorized them. I treated people in a special way because they are special. I treated people the way I like to be treated. Since new patients were coming to rehab, they were glad to see a friendly face that made them feel comfortable and welcome. This is just who I am.

One day I was caught off guard. I spoke to this lady and asked her how she was doing? She asked me why I kept speaking to her and she told me I was very annoying. Wow! I have been called many things in my life time, but I have never been called annoying. I listened to her explain to me why I annoyed her when I spoked to her all the time. I kept my smile and took it like a man. I couldn't wait to get home and tell my wife about this lady. My wife tried to play it off, however, I came up with a game plan. My game plan was very simple. I decided I would not speak to her anymore since I was so annoying. Meanwhile I continued to speak to everyone else as usual. After a few days, she recognized I was speaking to everyone except her. In my peripheral vision, I observed her with a sullen face. I was not rubbing it in and I was not trying to prove a point. I believed that being acknowledged frequently is much better than being ignored. What I wanted her to see was a friendly engaged environment brings about healing. Don't you agree?

## Prayer

As a former superintendent of a public charter school, I took the opportunity to pray with many parents going through different challenges with their kids. As the Chairman of the deacon board at my former church, I had the opportunity to pray with members of our church and visitors in our community. It is safe to say that prayer is a way of life for me. Some would say prayer changes things and I say prayer changes people also. Some would say it's a stress reliever, but I say it's the best reliever. At the clinic, I would initiate prayer when I felt it was needed and it was always well received. There was a day at rehab when I asked a patient how she was doing and she said terrible. I was caught off guard, so I asked her if I could pray with her and she blatantly said no. This was the first time I've been told not to pray. What do you do? I responded by saying, "I will be praying for you throughout the day as I was leaving the room. I saw her a couple times after that day. Three weeks later she saw me with a group of people and she approached me and asked me if I would pray for her? I asked if I could pray with her now? She said, she would love for me to pray with her. Obviously, she wasn't having any peace by shutting me out or by avoiding prayer.

Maybe I was annoying and maybe I shouldn't pray with some people. If that is the case, that goes against who I am and what I believe. That's not my personality, I would be a hypocrite. Eighteen months ago when I was admitted to therapy, I had one goal. My goal was to heal daily as I recover from my stroke. With my positive attitude and my relationship with Jesus Christ, I witnessed other patients being healed daily and recovering from their setbacks. Maybe I was a social butterfly but I saw several good things happening as I socialized. My friends and I are now walking and we have been delivered from the wheelchair. Now, I have a joy I cannot keep to myself. I have to tell somebody. I praise GOD for all that I've been through and I praise Him for not leaving me nor forsaken me during my challenging times. Great is thy faithfulness.

## Sympathy or Empathy

Empathy and sympathy are two words many people stumble over. Some people think the words are the same and I have seen people use them interchangeably. According to Meriam-Webster Dictionary, empathy and sympathy are homonyms but not synonyms. In other words, they sound similar but have different meanings. Empathy is the ability to understand and feel what another person is experiencing. Sympathy is the feelings of pity or sorrow for someone else's misfortune. (Merriam-Webster.com n.d.) As most of us recover from our stroke, our emotions go up and down like a roller coaster. No matter how strong or macho we used to be, we can't escape the inevitable. Patients recognize this fact and it is what it is, no excuses. Unfortunately, some therapists are out of the loop on how we feel at different times unless we have the opportunity to tell them. The reason this point is being made is because I can empathize with other stroke patients. Most people can sympathize but not all people can empathize. I take special pride in building people up with my love for Christ and my past experiences. There is no better way to comfort someone unless you have been comforted yourself. Experience is the best teacher.

## Open The Door

One day a young man, just learning to walk again, was getting out of the van to go inside The Centre for Neuro Skills. It was a cold windy day. I recognized from experience the man would have a difficult time opening the huge glass door so I beat him to the door and I opened it up for him. It sounds better if I said I ran to the door but that would be a lie because I can't run yet. He slowly made his way to the door as I held it open for him to walk into the building without a struggle. He showed his appreciation as he thanked me. I recognized his challenge to open the door in advance because one year ago from that day I was just barely walking. I had just started walking again with very little balance and that same door beat me up. I didn't fall down but it was a close call. I remember the struggle I had opening the door all by myself and when I was halfway through the door, the wind blew the door and it hit me in the rear. I was more startled and embarrassed than hurt. Since it was a scary moment and I could have been hurt, I wanted to make certain this man didn't have that same negative experience. At the clinic I not only sympathized and prayed with others but I also could empathize.

## Loud Music

Music was being played by a new patient while we were eating in our makeshift lunchroom area. At one time, all of us tried to eat in the regular cafeteria but for some reason or another, it didn't work out for us. It was about seven people or patients in our group that would always eat together in the front right quadrant of the Occupational Therapy (OT) room. There were another 6-8 patients scattered around the room and 6-8 helpers for all of us. People in our group had been at CNS from 5 to 15 months. I was the oldest and I had the most seniority of the group. Maybe that's why they treated me with much respect. I like to think it was because I was a Christian and I had much wisdom to offer. We all bonded prior to the Summer of 2022 and we ate in the OT area.

During lunchtime we had a great time and it was good therapy for all of us. In fact, this time was just as meaningful to us as our four therapy classes. We were very protective of each other. Most times we laughed and sometimes we got a little loud and even chastised by employees for being too loud, but I kept us in check most times. Maybe, I kept our noise under control because I observed two cameras above us recording all activities in that room. I saw this as being a good gesture. Sometimes we shared and even cried together while we were eating during our lunch hour. Since we all were at different stages of healing and recovery, it goes without saying that some of us were more sensitive or emotional than others. We were like a little community within a community. This music by the new patient was loud and annoying to us. One of the patients (new patient #1) in our group turned on his music to drain out the annoying music we had heard for days during our lunch hour. He was approached by two members of the staff on separate occasions to turn his music down. Both members were very kind and professional as they approached my friend. This was not the first time we played music, however it was the first time we were approached by two people on the same day to turn the music down.

The next day our friend (new patient #1) with the loud music decided to eat elsewhere because of yesterday's confrontation. I went to him and we talked about the incident. Yes, his feelings were hurt and he felt they were picking on him. This might not be a big deal outside the clinic but it is a major deal when you're recovering from a stroke and I have been there. I can empathize. I could feel his pain because I was in his position (stage of recovery) 7-8 months ago. By me being the unofficial president of our group, I felt inclined to have a kind word with the two different staff personnel. After praying, I approached them and my approach was very simple. The first thing I asked both of them was, can you do me a favor? I had been there for fifteen months and I had a good relationship with everybody. I wanted to be a peacemaker.

CNS is also known as a bridge to a meaningful recovery. I asked both of them to have a conversation with our friend. I didn't care what they talked about, it wasn't my business, but I felt a conversation would bring healing to this situation not just for now but also for the future for everybody. As you can imagine, people talk. So let's give them something positive to talk about. No one is right nor wrong, it's bigger than that. I took the initiative in making this happen because this is just who I am. I could have been told to mind my own business and that would have been okay pre-stroke but now I listen to no one but God when I'm advocating for unity and healing as we recover.

In other words, I'm being the bridge in CNS mission statement and I apologize to no one for doing what is right because it is the right thing to do. Everyone's feelings are important to them and we must be respectful of that. Sometimes we might not understand. Sometimes we must go over and beyond the call of duty to build people up even if we don't understand. During pre or post-stroke, most of us are sensitive people and our feelings do matter. Jesus says just like the Heaven are much higher than the Earth, so are His ways much higher than our ways and so are His thoughts much higher than our thoughts.

## The Almost Heavyweight Fight

Every day when I go to therapy is a blessing. I tell everyone this is the day that the Lord has made I will rejoice and be glad in it. I am blessed to be on top of the earth instead of the earth on top of me. Some days are normal and some days are more exciting. You never know what will be the highlight of the day. During our lunch hour, a member of our group had to go to the restroom. A young man in a wheelchair immediately took his place at the table. Some refer to him as a bully. Another patient (new patient #1) in a wheelchair in our group politely informed the man that the place was taken. The visitor said something back to our group member. I couldn't make out what the visitor was saying. Because of his tone and facial expression, I could tell it wasn't good. Apparently, the member of our group understood him clearly because he had very colorful cuss words to express back to the visitor and he finished by calling the man a bully and both of them were loud as they were facing each other exchanging words (profanity). They were toe to toe or should I say chair to chair. I thought to myself these young men in wheelchairs are about to fight.

One looked like Larry Holmes and the other one reminded me of Mike Tyson. Both of them were maybe 50-55 years old, close to 6'3" and 250lbs I thought to myself, I better get some help. But let me get my guy's attention (new patient #1) and calm him down first. I called his name and he gave me such a stare that made me feel intimidated and uncomfortable. I didn't know what to do so I started praying silently, then I stood up since I was the only one that could walk. Even though I couldn't run, I walked very fast to nowhere before another young man in a wheelchair came in our lunch area and called my friend (new patient #1) by his favorite name, "Lil Shit." My guy laughed hysterically when he heard this particular man call him this name and the almost heavyweight fight was over. God moves in mysterious ways.

CHAPTER 6

# Can't Hurry Healing – FaceBook Posts

During my recovery, I kept my friends and associates updated by social media. In fact, almost weekly, I posted something on Facebook. I wanted all of them to take the glorious journey with me and witness first-hand how God will heal and deliver me from my stroke. Faith without work is dead. Below are most of my posts in chronological order.

## #1 All Is Well

Hello: All is well. Thank you for checking! UPDATE: The shunt was placed at the top of his forehead to drain the cerebrospinal fluid (CSF) in the cavities (ventricles) of the brain to treat hydrocephalus (accumulation of fluid on the brain). Leroy has not lost any of his cognitive abilities. His thinking is sharp as ever. This part of the brain is the cerebellum, which affects speech, balance and swallowing. Through speech therapy, he will regain his speech. Through the continuous OT/PT, it will correct the balancing issue. Leroy is sitting up in the chair, everyday walking with OT/PT to increase his balance, less blood on the brain, eating more, less severe headaches, talking more and even singing, and very anxious to go home with his beautiful family. Please continue to pray for 100% and speedy recovery. Have a blessed day. His family are people of strong faith.

They have a group of people who are on the wall praying around the clock. They are holding on to Nehemiah 6:3 (NIV 2011) – paraphrase—they are not coming off the wall of prayer until 100% recovery for Leroy.

## #2 Best Patient I Can Be

Hello Facebook friends, Friday, August 20th was the first time I saw the outside since my stroke on July 30th. When I saw all of your support of prayers and beyond, it has given me more hope to live and fight for what God has called me to do. It has been a struggle! Talking and walking is now new to me.

Sometimes I feel like Apostle Paul when he says I feel hard pressed on all side but I'm not crushed, perplexed but not in despair, persecuted but not abandoned, shot down but not destroyed. (2 Corinthians 4:8-9) (NIV 2011) Despite my cognitive skills being intact, my # 1 goal is to walk again. I ask all of you to pray for my dry bones that I will walk out of rehab in God's timing. I am not in any hurry to go anywhere. My brothers and sisters, this is just a minor setback for a major comeback. Watch, pray and see what God will do through me as I recover.

The other day during rehab l tried to have a self-pity party but this strong-willed Black woman came in here and blessed me out. She initially used a few choice words and finished by quoting scripture and all I could do was say yes mam and Amen. You see, weeping may come at night but Joy comes in the morning. (Psalm 30:5) (NIV 2011) My oldest son, Shelton, has convinced me to lower my own expectations. My goal now is to be the best patient at this rehab so I can go home sooner and be with my family.

## #3 Let Your Light Shine!

When I came to this rehab I only had one thing in mind and that was when will I be able to walk again? I told every nurse and therapist of my goal was to be the best patient I could be so I can walk again. Most of them smiled and said I can't wait to work with you.

Despite being a CEO for over 20 years, I know how to be a good soldier. I know how to do what I am told, nothing more and nothing less. I knew 2 things going in. I had to be obedient before I received any blessings and my attitude would determine my outcome.

I was always introduced by my therapists as Mr. McClure and his goal is to be the best patient. Faith without works is dead. My work ethics is second to none. My dad taught me 50 years ago that laziness pays off now but hard work pays off for the future. A few therapists and patients have come to me and said the word around the rehab is I am a Rock Star. Can you believe that? I can barely talk and I can't dance so they are spreading that rumor. I do confess to signing a few books but l believe I know where all of this is coming from. Everywhere I go, individual therapy sessions or group sessions, I continue to think highly of others as I do myself. I catch myself comforting the new people that are distressed and building them up when they get emotional. When I was there during my first 2 days of therapy, the Lord comforted me. My situation is minor compared to others.

In the same way, let your light shine before others, that they may see your good deeds and glorify your Father in heaven. (Matthew 5:16) (NIV 2011)

If I'm a rock star, it's because of me allowing my light to shine everywhere. Blessings are all around me. You have to be present to see and feel the Holy Spirit working in this place.

In closing, my wife has been my greatest inspiration throughout all of my challenges. She keeps telling me how much I was improving every day. One day, I was exhausted after going through my therapy sessions, I made it to my room and Yvette was there like she has been every day. I usually stand up from my wheelchair all by myself, turn around and then sat in my bed. This day was different, I stood up from my wheelchair all by myself and Yvette said, "Lee, walk to me," and

I took a total of 9 steps and I walked to her. Maybe I walked because she commanded me to walk or maybe I walked because I knew there was a possibility if I reached her I could get more than a kiss this time.

I don't know how but I did it. I'm not making a big deal about it because God has other things for me to do while I'm here. I cannot put my light under a bowl. When I put it on a stand, it gives light to everyone that's here at the rehab. When I get a video of me walking again, we will talk then. Thanks for your continued prayers and more.

## #4 Dry Bones Coming to Life

On Monday 9-13-21, I transferred to another rehab facility from Encompass in Arlington for 21 days. They were great for me; I made great strides. They recommended Centre of Neuro Skills in Irving, a more advanced rehabilitation program for stroke victims. These people recognized my progress from Encompass and they loved me and put my butt to work. I was up for the challenge. After 1 week, now you see. Faith without work is dead! (James 2:26) (NIV 2011) I'm off to a good start. Believe me, I still have much work to do. Thanks to all of you for your prayers and more. Keep it coming. When God starts a good work in you, He will be faithful to complete it. Dry bones coming to life. God is able to do exceedingly and abundantly more than we think or ask in His power.

#healing. #faithandwork #Godisable

## #5 Hope and Faith

Hello my friends, some of you are either going through a storm, about to go through a storm or coming out of a storm. I can testify through it all, we need hope. Hope is getting me through my current storm.

It has been said that man can live for 40 days without food, 4 days without water, 4 minutes without air, but not 4 seconds without hope.

I met a young man the other day at my rehab who was in a snow skiing accident. His parents were in town from Atlanta

Georgia visiting him the other day. In fact, his mom introduced us to each other. He is in a wheelchair and not able to talk but he can communicate. He's only 16 years old and I've been led by the Spirit to find him every day at the Centre of Neuro Skills (rehab we attend) to speak to him and give him some dap. I have been told that my presence brightens up his day. All I try to do when I speak to him is offer him a little hope.

Leaders are responsible for providing hope to others, first, by setting down examples and second, by blessing others with their blessings.

"I know the plans I have for you," declares the Lord, "plans to prosper you and not to harm you, plans to give you hope and a future." Jeremiah 29:11 (NIV 2011)

I don't know yet if this young man knows the Lord or not, but if he hangs out with me long enough, I believe my faith will rub off on him.

By the way, I continue to get better. I still need to work on my balance, coordination, lower body strength and strength on my left side. I miss being home. It's been 55 days now since I have been home. Thank you for your prayers and more, they are still needed. We must finish strong.

#faith #hope #walkagain

## #6 Home Day Pass

After being away from home for 63 days from surgery and rehab, the Centre for Neuro Skills allowed me to come home for a day. It was a glorious time to finally be home with my family. For a quick minute I felt like a stranger because things have changed around the house in the last two months. Even with my sickness, it didn't take me long to recognize I'm still the head of my household when my family was treating me like a King. I thank God for my family and putting up with me through the good and bad. Without your prayers and more, I would not have been able to enjoy my 1-day home. I reach out to all of you to say "Thank You" for letting me get a glance of what Heaven can feel like with all of this love you continue to give. I got work to do. I need to get back to this rehab and put some work in. I'm making progress but I'm not there yet. I believe I will be home in less than 30 days.

## #7 No More Wheelchair

As of Friday, October 1, 2021; I quit using the wheelchair after being in it for 6 weeks because I couldn't walk. I now use the walker or I walk. Let me share a story with you about me going grocery shopping at Kroger in a wheelchair. Out of the 6 weeks I was in the wheelchair, I only went out in the public once and that was to go grocery shopping at Kroger. The Centre of Neuro Skills give us $75/week to buy groceries. Most of the time they give us a list and we write it down and they go and shop for you. This time I chose to go with them and do it myself. The young lady pulled the van in the first handicap parking space right next to Kroger front door. She got out and went to the back of the van to get my wheelchair. She brought it to the passenger side and I got out of the van and got into the wheelchair. Everybody were staring at me. This could be intimidating for most people but not for me. The stares continued throughout the store so I decided to have some fun with me getting all of this attention. As I was pushing myself down the aisle I saw this Black man staring at me so I said, "Excuse me young man, I noticed you staring at me. I'm a human being also and I am recovering from a stroke and now I'm in rehab and that's why I am in the wheelchair." He went on to ask me questions about my rehab and we dialogue for about 10 minutes. Everybody were staring at the man and me talking. As we were ending our conversation, I noticed a little Anglo boy riding in a bascart while his mom was pushing him. I turned the corner and found myself right behind the little boy and his mom. This mom has been trying to avoid me in the wheelchair ever since I entered the store. Now I'm right behind her and she was nervous and she was trying to speed up but the little boy in the bascart was slowing her down so she told the little boy to get down out of the bascart. The little boy started crying. I said, "Hey little man, you can ride with me." The little boy told his mom I want to ride with that man in the wheelchair. He said that at least 3 times while pointing at me. Mom ignored him as she was trying her best to get away from me while her little boy started screaming. "I want to ride with that man in that wheelchair." It was hilarious to say the least. The man in the wheelchair became popular.

If the truth be told, can we say most of us are guilty like some of those people I talked about when they were avoiding or staring at me in the wheelchair? I now know how to show more empathy and love for those in a wheelchair. After all, they are people too.

#wheelchair #empathy #rehab #humanity #love

## #8 Home Sweet Home

It was 90 days ago when I suffered a stroke. I could not walk. Today, I opened my gate and walked to my house. Ain't God good. My name is Leroy McClure, Jr. I can do All things with God's strength. I stated right after my brain surgery how this would play out. Faith without work is dead. There has been plenty of work and more to come. There has been plenty of praying and plenty of giving. Thanks for believing in me as we all believe that God can perform miracles. Maybe, you or a friend think this is a hoax. Transparency is the key to honesty. My family or I've kept you updated from the day I suffered a stroke.

I couldn't walk but now I'm able to walk over 1,000 feet. That's a miracle. God is able to do exceedingly and abundantly above all we can think or ask. Ephesians 3:20 (NIV 2011) My testimony is very simple. He is a miracle worker. I'm home now although I start out patient on Monday. Centre of Neuro Skills will pick me up at 7:30 am and bring me back at 3:00 pm, Monday-Friday. I will be taking classes such as physical therapy (PT), Occupational Therapy (OT), Cognitive Therapy (CT) and Speech or Education Therapy (ST, ET) 4 hours per day. They all have been a blessing to me just like you have. Please take this journey with me and let us experience God's will together. God has bigger plans for me, therefore I will rest and continue to heal.

## #9 Family Affair

My family came from Arkansas to visit me at home. They recognized not only I can walk but I now walk with a swag. I chose the swag over the robotic walk. More to come later. I figure if I was going to learn how to walk again, I might as well add a little style. I thank God daily for my family support and your support.

## #10 Let's Keep It Real

There are times when I have questions about my predicament and the pain I experience since I had my stroke. There are times when I'm angry with God. So I say this to let you know this journey has not been a slam dunk. It gets challenging at times and I can be lying in my bed at night where I can't figure out why my whole body is hurting. I call out to God and I realize it is because of His GRACE I can move and move on. Yes, I'm walking but I still have other issues that I don't care to talk about. Maybe you are going through some difficult times. Maybe you want God to relieve you from these issues. I have learned through my situation that He is not going to relieve me from my pain and anguish because He has a purpose, but I know His GRACE is sufficient. It is during my weakness when He is Strong. I ask for your prayers right now. Walking is great but I need more of God's GRACE. For those of you that are going through something right now, I pray that you will approach the Throne of Grace with Boldness and God will give you Grace and Mercy when you need it the most. Your brother in Christ. Leroy Jr.

## #11 Out Patient Therapy

I've been home for two weeks doing outpatient therapy at Centre of Neuro Skills (CNS) for five hours (including lunch) each day from Monday through Friday. Friday, my Physical Therapists (PT) took me to YMCA for 1.5 hours to ride the bike and do weights for my lower body. In order to get where I want to go, I must do what I haven't done. As I tell my story, I will continue to give God the Glory. I must not just focus on the destination without enjoying the journey. I enjoyed myself in the gym again but I have a new goal now. I'm trying to improve my balance, coordination and strength in my lower body. I'm trying to improve my walking so one day I can run again and walk with a swag. Meanwhile I will continue to get my rest and heal by taking my 90 minutes nap every day. This is very hard for me to do since I don't believe in taking a nap during business hours. The body is slowly healing and I will keep you posted every step of the way. Thanks for your prayers and more.

#rehab #recovery #faith #faithwithoutworkisdead.

## #12 I Praise God for My Progress

Before David fought Goliath, he praised God for delivering him from the paws of a lion and a bear. Every day, you and I have a challenge or a Goliath to deal with and we will win the battle with God's help.

Before David fought Goliath, he praised God for delivering him from the paws of a lion and a bear. Every day, you and I have a challenge or a Goliath to deal with and we will win the battle with God's help.

Before I talk about my next Goliath, let me boast how the Lord helped me defeat the lion and the bear in my life.

July 30- I had a stroke
For 6 weeks I couldn't walk. I was in a wheelchair.
For 2 weeks I used a walker

November 3, I was tested for a 6 min walk with a walker. I walked 700 feet.

November 15
Tested for 6 min walk with no walker or assistance.
I walked 1200 feet.

Today, according to my iPhone, I walk an average of 1 mile daily with no assistance.

I don't know what Goliath I have to face today, but I rebuke Satan in the name of Jesus and just like God delivered David from the paws of the bear and the lion, He will be with me when I face my next Goliath or challenge
.

#david&goliath #Godisgood #NoWeaponsFormedAgainstMeShallProsper

## #13 Cheerleader

There is a time for everything and a season for every activity under the Heaven. Ecclesiastes 3:1 (NIV 2011)

The other day I walked into the Physical Therapy room. I sat down and looked across the room. I noticed six empty wheelchairs while the patients were working with the Physical Therapists. I thought to myself, I was in the same position as these patients
six weeks ago doing the same exercise, etc., I wonder if they really believe everything is going to be alright if they keep grinding. I kept thinking to myself, for a season I use to be a basketball player but now I m a cheerleader. I enjoy encouraging all of the patients to keep up the good work despite the aches and pain and that everything is going to be alright. Just look at me, I'm a living example. I was in the wheelchair but now I'm walking. Praise God! There is a time and season for everything under the heavens.
#praiseGod

## #14 Strokes of Love

My sister-in-law lives in Little Rock, Arkansas with her husband. She had a stroke exactly one week before I had my stroke. Her stroke affected her differently than the way I was affected by my stroke. I was mostly affected physically but not her. I was in the wheelchair but she was not. During Thanksgiving week, she came to stay with us because the best services for stroke victims are here in the metroplex of Dallas. She goes to rehab with me every day. We are picked up Monday-Friday at 7:30 AM and brought home at 3:00 pm by The Centre for Neuro Skills (CNS) in Irving, TX. We both are headed for a full recovery but it will take some time. One day at a time. She has already seen progress.

I love spending time and recovering with my sister-in-law. I, also, love meeting new patients at CNS weekly encouraging them with agape love.

The clinic (CNS) asked me to be on a newcomer committee. This is confirmation that I am right where I should be while doing what I supposed to be doing. In closing, my message to you is whatever you are doing in life right now, do it like you are doing it for the Lord. Wherever you are in life, God will meet you there and He will help you get through it if you let him. My God is real! Please keep praying for me and my sister-in-law as we recover together. Thanks #stroke #agapelove #CNS #beencouraged

## #15 I'm Back Ready for Rehab

Last week was a difficult week for me because I couldn't be around anyone. I tested positive for COVID-19. Despite not having any symptoms, I only went to get tested because I was around someone who tested positive with COVID-19. I'm grateful that I've been vaccinated and I had my booster shot and I was never sick. I was in quarantine for 10 days to keep from spreading the virus. Monday I get to continue my rehab and be around people. I encourage all of you to get vaccinated and get tested. Take this COVID-19 virus seriously. Even if you are not sick but been around someone that tested positive, go and get tested. We all must stop the spread of this Virus because some people are not vaccinated and their health might not be able to withstand this virus.

Another thing, let's quit being secretive. It appears no one has COVID-19 until you tell them about your situation. Then they will say something like, I believe I had COVID-19 last week or my family had the virus. Quit being secretive, let us get vaccinated, tested and save lives.

## #16 I Am Better Not Bitter

What is your excuse? I had a stroke. There were days when I asked God, why me?

I would get bitter, but not for long. His answer was always the same. God replied in a soft voice, "Why not you, with my help you can handle this. I have a plan for you, but you must let go." Initially, I had no idea what He was talking about when He said you must let go. After 6 months, it is now crystal clear. One thing He was telling me to let go was some of my friends. I don't have much time these days to talk to all friends so now I choose wisely. Not all friends are genuine.

Friends, are they your friends or are you their friend? Some friendships are toxic. If the truth be told, some of your friends are toxic. It could be your so called best friend or your cousin. I had a stroke and I have slowed down, I'm no longer in a hurry. I have plenty of life left. I see things in people I couldn't see before, good and bad. I now have some new friends. Some of them are in a wheelchair. I spend most of my time healing and getting prepared for my purpose on earth. If it's not positive, I cut it out of my life. No excuses! Not only am I on the road to recovery, but I'm better, not bitter. What about you?

#better. #bitter #friendship #stroke #valueadded

## #17 Laughter

Many of us need to laugh more often, Laugh Therapy. As I go through rehab, it's imperative for me to not leave out laughter. The Bible says laughter is like good medicine. Proverbs 17:22 (NIV 2011) The other day I laughed for three hours. I didn't say I worked out for 3 hours, I laughed for three hours by listening to this very clean comedian, Michael Jr. is his name. He's more than funny and he's clean. I found him on YouTube. I highly recommend Michael Jr. and please tell me what you think.

#laughter. #michaeljr.

## #18 Faithwalk

As I continue to improve my walking, I'm reminded that I wasn't walking just a few months ago. I have increased my daily walking up to 2.25 miles or 5,700 steps per day. Faith without work is dead. We all need to stop talking and start walking. Our health depends on it. My goal is to learn how to run again. What's yours?

Youth grow tired and weary. Young men may stumble and fall. But those that wait upon the Lord will renew their strength, they will soar on the wings like an eagle. They will run and not grow weary and they will walk and not faint. Isaiah 40:31 (NIV 2011)

#faith #faithwalk #rehab. #finishstrong.

## #19 Obedience before Blessings

Most people want something for nothing. As Christians, we sometimes mistake God for Santa Claus. We say a little prayer then we expect God to deliver. Have you been obedient to God's words, statues, commandments, decrees, precepts or laws? Let's not get it twisted, He doesn't answer everybody's prayers according to their desire. He is not a 9-1-1 operator. We must get right (salvation) with God first, become Obedient then Blessings overflow. Most people know their ABC's and the letter B comes before the letter O, but in the spiritual world, the letter O comes before the letter B. You must be Obedient before there is a Blessing! I walked 4 miles the other day because I have been obedient by getting up 30 minutes early to practice walking before I go to rehab each morning since March 7, 2023. I now average 3.1 miles/day or 7,500 steps/day. Don't forget in August and September I was in a wheelchair, I couldn't walk.

Quit being a fan and get in the game of life. Be OBEDIENT then BLESSINGS will overflow. Hallelujah!

#obedient #blessings

## #20 Be Grateful

The other day a young lady approached me and said Mr. McClure, I read your book, The Shot Doctor: Nothin' But Net. Can you teach me how to shoot a basketball? I replied by saying, I would love to, but first I must teach myself how to walk like a king, (not like a robot), how to stand on one leg, how to walk on grass, how to step up on a curb, how to step down from a curb, how to walk up and down an incline, how to walk backwards, how to turn around in a circle, how to skip, how to shuffle sideways, how to go up and down the stairs using the side rail, how to get in and out of a car and how to dance again. Once I teach myself all of these things, I would love to teach you how to shoot a basketball; however, I must teach myself first.

Let's be grateful for where we are and let's not take life for granted. I Praise God daily for my 2 eyes, 2 feet, 2 legs, 2 arms, 2 hands with 10 fingers, 2 ears, a nose, a mouth and I'm still handsome.

Basketball has been a big deal for me and my family for over 50 years, but for NOW, it's the small things that matter most. That resurrection power that raised Jesus from the dead will also help me to do all of those small things I once took for granted and I will even become the Shot Doctor again in God's timing.

Romans 8:28 says all things work together for the good for those who love Him and called according to His purpose. (NIV 2011) Thanks my FB friends for your continued prayers and more. Jesus has risen and I am rising!

#Hehasrisen.
#Godisonthethrone
#begrateful

## #21 Run Leroy Run

Wednesday morning at 6:30 am., Yvette and I were working out in our gym. I was walking fast and she asked me if I was running? I said no but let me see if I can. So I took off and ran. Yes, I ran for the first time since my stroke. This is a miracle!

Youth grow tired and weary
Young man may stumble and fall but those that wait on the Lord will renew their strength
They will soar on the wings of an eagle
They will RUN and not grow weary and
They will WALK and not faint. Isaiah 40:31 (NIV 2011)
#stroke #run #miracle

# CHAPTER 7

# On The Road and Driving Again

**Driving Simulator**

    I ran over two children while they were riding their bikes on the side of the street. This happened when I was in a driving simulator class after about seven months of therapy. I was affected severely in an emotional way. I wanted to get the phone number of the parents to tell them how sorry I was for running over their children while I was driving. It took me almost three months before I could go back into that driving simulator room again. I know it sounds silly but to me at the time, it was real. Because of this experience, I was not interested in driving again. I had a fear. I decided I would be chauffeured for the rest of my life. I gave up on driving. Giving up was out of character for me: therefore, I needed to get a handle on this quickly. I don't care if I am sick or not, I am not a quitter. I have spent my entire life teaching people not to quit. Winners never quit and quitters never win.

## Driving in The Neighborhood

A few months later my youngest son, King took me to the barber to get a haircut. While driving back home, I asked him to pull over into this new neighborhood, stop and let me drive. He was quite surprised and compliant simultaneously. We traded places. I was the driver and he was the passenger. I needed to prove to myself that I could drive so that's why I chose this new neighborhood. I felt really good and comfortable while I was driving in this neighborhood. Apparently, my son thought I was driving really good also because he secretly videoed me while I was driving. Finally, I told him I was going to drive home and he was okay with that.

I drove out of the new neighborhood to the main highway. I first allowed several cars to pass by before I merged on to the main highway with more than a dozen cars. I drove over four miles and I approached two traffic lights the proper way without a problem before I made it home. When I drove onto the driveway to my house, my youngest daughter, Princess was outside waiting for us. Initially, I couldn't understand why she was waiting and then I discovered my son was videotaping me and sharing it with her. Apparently, she and all the people that follow my son saw me on Instagram.

As soon as I got into the house and sat down in my recliner, I received a phone call from a coach friend of mine. He was congratulating me for my good driving. He knew too much: therefore, I asked him if he was following behind me when I was driving. He said no but my son posted it on Instagram. Needless to say, I can drive now without any fear. Jesus says He did not give us a spirit of fear, but a spirit of love, a spirit of power and a sound mind. FEAR stands for False Evidence Appearing Real. I beat this fear or phobia with the help of my family.

I chose not to drive on a regular basis until I was done with rehab. Maybe it's because I misplaced my driver's license and I will use that time to slow down, stay focus and enjoy my family while I wait for my replacement license to come in. This will be during the Summer.

## Family Affair

Post stroke, I've come to realize that family support comes in different forms, different shapes and different ways. It's not just about what your family can do for you but what can you and your family do together so that crucial or meaningful conversations can take place. During pre-stroke it appeared in my family, everyone was always going in different directions. I'm so proud of my children since they all have finished college and have become young productive Christian adults. During late summer of 2022, my teammates and I on our 1976 basketball team with a record of 36-0 were inducted into Conway High School Sports Hall of Fame.

My youngest son and daughter agreed to drive my wife, Yvette and I to the Hall of Fame Banquet in Conway Arkansas. It was a five-hour trip. My son King was driving and my daughter Princess was riding in the passenger seat while Yvette and I were sitting in the back. This was a first. For 20 years, the seating arrangements were reversed. Since I have had a stroke, it has been very difficult for me to get my son King on the phone, even though he has strong ADHD symptoms. Sometimes I just want to know if he is okay since he travels across the country and the world. I know he's busy and he has his own career with ESPN but when I call, I need him to answer, call back or text me in a timely manner. I have raised him up much better than that so I thought. This might not be a big deal to you but inside of me this was killing me softly. I needed to have this crucial uninterrupted conversation with him.

Since we were going to be with each other in the same car for five hours on this trip, this is the time. To be honest, this has been a pet peeve of mine even before my stroke. Post stroke, I need to go for it and I apologize to no one when I'm hurting inside and can't hold my peace. It took me an hour before I made my first move. That time was used to observe him answering his phone and not answering his phone when it would ring. So I started the conversation by asking King when do you decide to answer your phone? He replied by saying when it is my agent or my family, I always answer my phone. I balked for five seconds, then I said "that's a damn lie". I literally shocked him. He was stunned because he has never heard me talk like that. He was shocked because I was telling the truth and I was confronting him at the same time. It was silence in the car for the next five minutes. Maybe he really believed that lie or he wanted that to be true. Even though I felt bad for using such bad or strong language, I got his undivided attention. I apologized later and ask him and Jesus for forgiveness.

I felt like this was the right time so I seized the moment. When leaders fail to seize the moment, they undermine their leadership. I shared my heart with him and I unconsciously mentioned my stroke. I shared what my expectations were when I called him and why. It was a 15-20-minute emotional speech and it was well received. He made a commitment to do better. I told him I would hold him to it. As we drove for another hour it was absolutely quiet. So I broke the silence by calling King on his phone. He glanced at his phone, looked at me through his rearview mirror and then picked up his phone to answer it. I said, "Hello King, I see you are busy. I'll talk to you later". He hung the phone up and probably wandered what's going on with his dad. I immediately thanked King for answering his phone and I made it a big deal. I told him he was doing so much better and now he was 1 for 1. An hour later, I called him again and he looked at his phone, looked in his rear view mirror again, saw me, then he answered. I again said, "King, this is your dad, are you tired from driving? Thanks for answering your phone". He politely nodded his head and said, "You are welcome". I made a big deal out of this. I praised him and told him how proud his mom and I were of him. I told him he was 2 for 2 and he was a man of his words. Between that day and the next day, I called my son eight to ten times and he answered every single time.

This moment of accomplishment was greater than being inducted into my high school hall of fame. Eight months later, I had called or text King more than 100 times and he answered or responded back every single time in a timely manner. He's still at 100% answering my phone calls or getting back to me.

In conclusion, before my stroke, my busyness would not have allowed my two youngest children to drive us to my Hall of Fame

Banquet with my wife and I in the backseat. Therefore, that crucial conversation would not have happened and those multiple follow up phone calls would not have been necessary. Accountability should be embraced as our friend and not as our enemy if done in a loving way. All of this happened post stroke. Life is good: I'm now better not bitter.

## CNS: A Life Saving Therapy Presentation

Figure 3: The ABC's Life Saving Therapy presentation at CNS

In August 2022, I had an opportunity to do a presentation for the patients and staff in the cafeteria. It was well attended. It was packed, only standing room was available. The presentation was on the topic, The ABC'S OF LIFE SAVING THERAPY. I had a great time presenting and I was in a zone. I talked about how your ATTITUDE will determine your success in therapy and how my attitude was second to none. In fact, I told every therapist my goal was to be the best patient I could be. Second, I told them they must BELIEVE in themselves, their therapists, their counselors and a higher being. I believed in Jesus also. Lastly, I told them they must CARRY their own load. This is not the time to be lazy. There is no substitute for hard work. Laziness pays off now but hard work pays off for the future. I told them when I first came to CNS, I was in a wheelchair and I couldn't walk but now I take over 8,000 steps each day and I had taken over 1 million steps at that time. Faith without work is dead. My presentation was easy to give because this is what I believed and it was who I am. I just gave them a synopsis of my life post stroke.

## Left Side Rehab

Rehabilitation for my left side, coordination and my balance is now needed after 18 months since my stroke. I spent so much time and work in learning to walk again that it appeared I had forgotten about my left shoulder, left arm, left hand, balance and coordination. Rehab is needed for all of them. I didn't really forget about them, I had to prioritize which one mattered the most. Now that I'm walking, my left side has my full undivided attention. I had a difficult time putting my shirt on and taking it off because I couldn't raise my left arm above my head without excruciating pain. Therefore, my wife helped me put on and take off my shirt every day for several weeks until I was able to strengthen my left arm and shoulder with exercises and by lifting weights at Coppell Family YMCA.

I also had a difficult time holding things including a basketball because of the excruciating pain from my three middle fingers on my left hand. I had difficulty hitting the rim when shooting a basketball while under the goal. I could hit the basket when shooting with only my right hand but not if I shot a basketball the correct way. The correct way is using two hands, left hand holding the ball up while the right hand is shooting the ball. This is important to me because I am known as the Shot Doctor and I cannot shoot a basketball right now. In fact, I haven't picked up a ball in 18 months. I'm the author of the book, "The Shot Doctor: Nothin' But Net." In this book, I share the four components of how to shoot a basketball and how I taught my son to be one of the best shooters in the country during 2015, his senior year in high school.

For 90 days I've used different exercises, activities and weights to strengthen my left arm. Now I'm able to put my shirt on and take it off all by myself. I can raise both arms over my head. It's a slow process but I am seeing progress. I have much hope on my recovery. Hope is powerful!

It has been said that man can live for 40 days without food, 4 days without water, 4 minutes without air, but not 4 seconds without hope.

## Basketball: The Shot Doctor Comeback

The Shot Doctor is coming back. I went into my gym the other day and I finally made one free throw after taking about 25 shots or more. I shot the ball the correct way without any pain. Remember a free throw is 15 feet from the basketball rim. The basketball rim is 10 feet high from the floor. Prior to my stroke, I could make 8 out of 10 free throws consistently. Once, I made 55 consecutive free throws. My goal is to improve my accuracy despite now taking 25 attempts to make 1 shot.

My challenge is to shoot the ball without falling as I raise the ball up with both hands using the left hand with my three index fingers in pain if I apply too much pressure to them. Because of these sensitive fingers on my left hand, I certainly can't dribble a basketball ball with the left hand without excruciating pain. While shooting, the left hand holds the ball in place long enough for my right hand to shoot it. As you see, much thought goes into shooting a basketball ball now. Much thought goes into my walking. Much thought goes into me not falling when I walk and when I shoot the basketball. Much thought goes into grabbing the ball and then standing.

This is my new normal. I'm okay with it all because my Lord has given me hope and my faith is strong. Jesus tells us to lean not on our own understanding but in all our ways acknowledge Him and He will direct our path. Each week I would go into my gym to see if I could make more free throws. The second week, I made 5 free throws. The third week, I made 10 free throws. The fourth week, I made 15 free throws. The fifth week, I made 20 free throws. The sixth week, I made 25 free throws. The seventh week, I made 30 free throws. The eighth week, I made 35 free throws. The ninth week, I made 40 free throws. The tenth week, Super Bowl LVII weekend, I made 50 free throws. On the eleventh week, I made 60 free throws. On the twelfth week, I made 75 free throws, I also made 90 free throws two days later. On the thirteenth week, I made 100 free throws. On March 14 2023, I made 31 out of 50 free throws and continued shooting over 50% everyday all the way through June.

As I finish writing this book, you can see every week I was getting better. I did all of this all by myself without using a rebounder. A rebounder would immediately give me the ball back after I shot it. I would never have to leave the free throw line by having a rebounder. He would retrieve the ball for me. From the beginning, I missed more free throws than I made. All shots must be retrieved but missed shots must be chased down then picked up. Some missed shots ended up at the other end of the court. I would have to walk 50-75 feet to retrieve the ball before I could shoot another free throw. Bending down, grabbing the ball with two hands, picking it up while standing up without losing my balance to fall down was a challenge for me. I could get a rebounder but I chose not to. It's not time yet. I needed the workout.

You have to understand I love the game of basketball. Behind my love for Jesus Christ, my wife and family, basketball is my third love. My family and I love the game so much that when I built my house in 2006, I built a full basketball court in the house. I trained my son to be one of the best basketball players in the country before he went to college. For a season, my gym was not being used, it was dormant. Now, it's a season for rehab. I'm able to use my gym for rehab and I enjoy working out just to get myself back close to normal. I didn't mind chasing the basketball down so I could shoot more free throws.

Walking to get the ball was therapy. Picking the ball up without hurting my left hand was therapy. Standing up after bending down was therapy. Walking with the ball to the free throw line without falling was therapy. I enjoyed all of this because every step of the process was therapy and it was good for my recovery. I would not shortcut the process for the same reason you wouldn't use scissors to help a butterfly get out of its cocoon. Struggle is necessary for progress.

## The Lesson of the Butterfly

A man spent hours watching a butterfly struggling to emerge from its cocoon. It managed to make a small hole, but its body was too large to get through it. After a long struggle, it appeared to be exhausted and remained absolutely still.

The man decided to help the butterfly and, with a pair of scissors, he cut open the cocoon, thus releasing the butterfly. However, the butterfly's body was very small and wrinkled and its wings were all crumpled.

The man continued to watch, hoping that, at any moment, the butterfly would open its wings and fly away. Nothing happened; in fact, the butterfly spent the rest of its brief life dragging around its shrunken body and shriveled wings, incapable of flight.

What the man – out of kindness and his eagerness to help – had failed to understand was that the tight cocoon and the efforts that the butterfly had to make in order to squeeze out of that tiny hole were Nature's way of training the butterfly and of strengthening its wings.

Sometimes, a little extra effort is precisely what prepares us for the next obstacle to be faced. Anyone who refuses to make that effort, or gets the wrong sort of help, is left unprepared to fight the next battle and never manages to fly off to their destiny. (Coelho 2021)

This is why I wouldn't use a rebounder until four or five months. By then; I would be making over 80% of my free throws. Coelho 2021

Consider it pure joy my brother, the various trials you may encounter. The testing of your faith produces endurance. Endurance causes you to be more perfect, more mature and more complete, lacking in nothing. James 1:2-4

As you can see the progress in me shooting free throws, I desire to see similar progress in other areas of my life as I identify that area. It is not about getting back to normal; it's about making as much progress as possible with a way of measuring the progress. I continued to improve my shooting at the free throw line. In March 2023, I started shooting 50 free throws every morning Monday through Friday. In the month of March, I averaged shooting 55% from the free throw line, In April I averaged shooting 65% from the line. In May, I averaged 72%. My accuracy continued to improve as I shot free throws each morning. In June I started shooting only 10 free throws each morning. I went 9-10 the first day and 8-10 the second day.

## Basketball: Free Throws Made-Attempts

### March. 2023

3-14-23 31-50
3-15-23. 26-50
3-16-23. 42-75
3-18-23. 26-50
3-20-23 26-50
3–21-23. 36-50
3-22-23. 32 -55
3-23-23. 27-50
3-24-23. 34-50
3-25-23. 43-75
3-27-23. 28-50
3-28-23 30-50
3-29-23. 30- 50
3-30-23. 33-50
3-31-23. 27 50

**March 442-805 55%**

### April 2023

4-03-23. 25-50
4-04-23. 31-50
4-05-23. 36-50
4-06-23. 34-50
4-07-23. 28-50
4-10-23. 35-50

4-11-23. 35-50
4-12-23. 34-50
4-17-23. 32-50
4-18-23. 39-50
4-19-23. 28-50
4-20-23. 35-50
4-21-23. 34-50
4-24-23. 35-50
4-25-23. 19-20
4-26-23. 33-50
4-27-23. 28-50
4-28-23. 34-50

**April 575-870
66%**

**May**

5-01-23. 33-50
5-02-23. 36-50
5-03-23. 38-50
5-04-23. 35-50
5-05-23. 40-60
5-08-23. 38-50
5-09-23. 37-50
5-10-23. 43-60
5-11-23. 39-50
5-12-23. 31-50
5-15-23. 37-50
5-16-23. 33-50
5-17-23. 35-50
5-18-23. 36-50
5-19-23. 37-50
5-22-23. 30-50
5-23-23. 37-50
5-24-23. 36-50

5-25-23. 40-50
5-26-23. 37-50
5-29-23. 34-50
5-30-23. 38-50
5-31-23. 42-50

**May 842-1170**
**72%**

**June**

**6-06-23 9-10**
6-07-23 8-10
6-08-23 7-10
6-09-23 7-10
6-12-23 9-10
6-13-23 10-10
6-14-23 6-10
6-15-23 8-10
64-80

**June**
**80%**

## Resurrected to Jog

 Easter weekend was very special for me. At CNS, I'm doing 995. I am very close to 1,000. The day after Easter, Resurrection Sunday, I learned how to jog, you know like running. A young lady from CNS California office came to work in the PT department for one week. She worked my butt off. I could tell from the beginning of therapy she did not play and she was the real deal. After 40 minutes of therapy she asked me if I knew how to jog and I quickly told her no. She disagreed and said "let's jog". For the next ten minutes I jogged.

As a Christian, I believe I have the same power that resurrected Jesus from his grave on Easter Sunday. As I was jogging on Monday, I made certain everyone that could hear my voice, saw me jogging. I was overwhelmed with emotions. During the end of Summer 2023, I jogged ½ mile more than once. It's moments like this that give me the power to believe with God's help I can do all things.

## Coppell Family YMCA

Centre for Neuro Skills (CNS) transports some of their patients to Coppell Family YMCA (CFYMCA) to work out in their gym. I believe this YMCA is one of the best YMCA in the state of Texas. I was very fortunate to be one of those patients. My first trip to the gym was very interesting. After getting out of the wheelchair, I initially had a difficult time getting on the van. That alone was a workout for me. Getting on the van and getting off the van was a big challenge for me. The staff and gym members at CFYMCA were very kind to us as we worked out. I don't know why I was chosen to go to the gym because I could barely walk. Pre-stroke, I stayed in the gym on a daily basis, but now I'm trying to figure out if going to the gym would be part of my future or if it was part of my old life. At the time I was too weak to lift weights and the left side of my body was hurting: therefore, all I did was walk upstairs on the track. Fourteen laps around the track equals a mile. I walked 7 laps around the track and then I went up and down the steps three to four times and I would finish by getting on the stationary bike for 40 minutes. I averaged taking over 8,000 steps each day.

I went to the YMCA on Monday, Wednesday and sometimes Friday. I made friends with many people while I was working out. Many people were curious about our group and I felt like a CNS ambassador telling them about the great things happening at CNS and how my life is so much better since my stroke.

I am like a social butterfly so I talked to everyone who looked at me and smiled. It was obvious to me these new friends were intrigued to hear my story because each time I appeared, more people were wanting to talk with me. I could tell they all have been talking about me in a good way. My story is simple. I had a stroke. I had a minor setback for a major comeback. These members at Coppell Family YMCA were about my age, 50's and 60's. All of them had interesting conversations. I had so many complements on my positive attitude. Just that statement alone can conjure up a 25-minute conversation.

My entire life is an open book. I could teach a lesson, preach a sermon, inspire a team or write a book based on chapters of my life and my newly acquired friends witnessed this first hand. I absolutely loved these people who were genuine and transparent. My goal was for them to look pass my ethnicity and see Jesus in me. My conversation with them was part of my healing. I was so excited because everyone I spoke with was quick to compliment me on my progress. One day, I had many compliments when my friends saw me running on the track. They were more excited about my progress than I was. It wasn't that I was not excited, it's more like I'm so focused on the destination that it took my new friends to remind me to stop and celebrate the journey sometimes. For some of my new friends, I might be the only Black man they speak to on a frequent basis and that's okay because agape love is color blind. The great thing about my experience at CFYMCA is all things work together for the good for those who love the Lord and called according to his purpose. (Romans 8:28, NIV 2011) Like Apostle Paul said, I am not ashamed of the gospel because the power of God bring salvation to everyone who believes: first to the Jews and then the Gentiles. One year and a half after being at the YMCA, I found that running on the track and lifting weights to build up my left side helped me appreciate how much I had missed being in the gym during my temporary setback.

CHAPTER 8

# Milestones Something Worth Talking About

**Born to Lose**

Figure 5 Hat-Born to Lose

Yes, you heard me. Now, let me tell you the whole story. I had been attending class with this 24-year-old man with extremely long hair handsome young man. Every conversation he had with me or anyone was always negative. I heard him say when he had a motorcycle accident, he lost everything. When he had to go to the hospital, he lost his girlfriend, he lost his baby girl and he lost his trailer. He went on to say more then he finished by saying he was a born loser. I wanted to intervene but the class adjourned. I prayed silently that I could finish this conversation with this young man at a later time. The next day, this young man was in my Physical Therapy class. I overheard him telling a friend of mine the same nonsense he had been sharing to anyone that would listen: therefore, I jumped into the conversation quickly. My friend was trying to shed positive light on him. I said young man, we all are here because of a crisis. We have decided to move forward and make the most out of our adversity. He interrupted me by saying but I'm a born loser. My friend asked me to look at the back of his hat. The back of his hat read, "BORN TO LOSE". After reading the back of his hat, I told him "tomorrow, I will bring you a new Nike hat and you and I will switch hats. Okay". He agreed. I couldn't wait to see him the next morning. Interestingly, while I was looking for him, he was looking for me. We switched hats and he was a happy young man. He went on to tell everyone what happened. I mean everyone including patients, therapists and counselors. He now had a new story to tell. I didn't know this man's whole story but I knew enough to give him hope.

Proverbs 23:7 says, So a man think it in his heart so is he.

## Memorial Weekend

Memorial Weekend in 2022 was an interesting and challenging weekend for me. All I wanted to do is barbecue. I'm known for my good barbecue, however, it has been almost a year since I have put meat on the grill. The weather was beautiful so my adult children went to the store and bought me a new grill since they love my barbecue. I do my barbecue with 90% pecan wood and 10% charcoal. Usually I make a fire good enough to last for 5 hours.

Early Sunday morning, my wife and I started gathering wood from the pecan trees in the front yard. This use to be simple but now it's a real job. We picked up branches that had fallen from the trees. Most of the branches were longer than the grill so I needed to make them shorter. This is a problem. I use to step on the branches and break them with my foot. I told Yvette this so she tried to do it but it didn't work. I went to get my chainsaw but the chain came off so I couldn't use it.

I have five long branches too long to put in my grill to barbecue so I went inside to pray and regroup. Before my stroke, this has never been an issue. After 20 minutes in the house, I told Yvette to get the keys and get in the car. I had her to run over the branches with the car. All branches snapped into two pieces. I proceeded and started my fire. It was a good fire that lasted five hours.

I barbecued baby back ribs. Country styles ribs, Earl Campbell links, Earl Campbell Cheddar Cheese links, chicken wings, chicken legs, chicken breasts and hot dogs. Historically. I always grilled enough meat for 30 people and this day was no different. Fortunately, a few friends of King, stopped by and stayed over for the weekend and they were hungry. These guys were tall ranging from 6'3" to 6'10" (NBA players) and they couldn't get enough of my barbecue. This time, barbecuing wore me out after five hours. In the past, I would get in 1,000 push-ups during this time. My son King and my wife, Yvette took two more hours to finish the barbecue. My stroke allowed me to see that as of right now, I must approach my love for barbecuing differently until I build my stamina. It's no longer fun, it's now work.

Today is Memorial Day, May 30, 2022. I'm doing 525 at CNS. My outlook on life is very positive but my ability to go back to work and perform at my highest level is still to be desired. I still have issues on my left side, left arm and hand, my balance and coordination. I should not be focusing on my situation when I should be focusing on Christ Jesus who control all of what is happening in me and to me or else I will put myself into a negative funk if I keep thinking about what I can and cannot do. Either way, God is working everything out for my good, according to His specific purpose. The key to accepting the truth to God's unconditional love is to focus attention on Him rather than my circumstances. When you are learning of Him, talking with Him, and sharing your life with Him, trust and faith will replace fear and doubt.

## It's My Birthday - June 22, 1960

Sixty-two years ago a star was born and God said I was wonderfully and marvelously made. This birthday was my most appreciated birthday. I am so grateful to see 62 years young. I have never been big at celebrating my birthdays in the past. This year's birthday was so special because I almost didn't make it through the stroke on July 30, 2021 according to man. God has something to say about that because He is not done with me yet. CNS is doing an excellent job in preparing me for the work God has for me to complete. God says when He started a good work in me, He will be faithful to complete it. Philippians 1:6 (NIV 2011) Praise God!

## Charity

CNS does many good things in the state of Texas and one of them is giving back to the Community. On Thursday, the Occupational Therapist Department Head takes myself and other patients to do volunteer work at a food bank in south Dallas. Private schools and nonprofit organizations also have their students and employees doing volunteer work at this food bank. The food bank name is Aunt Bette's Community Pantry and it is owned by the prestigious St. Phillips Episcopal School located at 1600 Pennsylvania Avenue.

Twenty-five to thirty-years ago, this neighborhood had one of the highest crime rates in the state of Texas. The Headmaster has brought academic excellence to the hood. As an educator, I've worked on several projects with the Headmaster, who is a brilliant man of impeccable character.

I thought one day I would run into him, however, I must remember I was there to work on my fine and gross motor skills as I did volunteer work at the food bank. One Thursday, we walked into the food bank and guess who I saw? Yes, I saw the Headmaster and he was giving some VIPs a tour of the food bank.

I noticed him first and he didn't recognize me with my face mask and hair with locks. Once I took my mask off he recognized me and wanted to know what I was doing there? I briefly shared my story with him and he was taken back and was not aware of my stroke. He made sure he still had my contact information in his phone and he said that he had a copy of my book, Why Sammy Still Can't Read and he liked it. People in the food bank were listening to our conversation: therefore, many of them recognized despite my impairment from my stroke, I also might be very important. When it's God's will, I will be back to doing what I love to do, teaching people how to turn adversity in to victory, how to turn problems into opportunities and how to be a winner in a losing situation. This is who I am, the real Leroy McClure, Jr.

## One Summer Day

During the hot summer of July 2022 in Texas, I needed to put a license plate on the front bumper of my car. The back license plate was easy because the plastic bumper had two holes in it and they aligned up with the two holes in the license plate. All I had to do was to get two screws and I screwed the plate to the hard plastic bumper. It took less than five minutes to put the back plate on. Now the front plate was more challenging because I only had one hole in the hard plastic bumper to work with. Therefore, I needed to put a second hole in the plastic bumper that would align with the two holes in the license plate. As I proceeded, I recognized I didn't have a drill and my screws were only 3/4-inch-long, too short for me to hammer one in to create a hole since I kept hitting my thumb as I was hammering. I couldn't get a hole into the hard plastic.

I thought about quitting for many reasons but I refused to let this outcome be my new normal. I recognized my screws were too short for creating a hole so I left the hot temperature of 104 degrees to enter into the air condition house to find a longer sharp screw. My wife directed me to longer screws then I went back outside to complete the job. I bent over slightly to hammer in the longer screw just to create a hole but my balance and equilibrium was off. Because it was hot and I was tired, I went back into the air condition house to rethink my little project that had taken 25 minutes so far. After discussing my situation with my wife, she recommended me to pull up a chair to the front bumper and sit in it while hammering the screw into the bumper. Finally, the hole was created, now I needed a screw driver. I went into the house to get one and I finished the project 35 minutes after I started. I'm okay with this because I finished what I started and this could be my new normal.

## A Shining Light

Jesus says the devil comes to kill, steal and destroy but He has come so we may have life and have life more abundantly. John 10:10 (NIV 2011) I can't talk to you about a heart attack because I have never had one. I can't speak on cancer because I have never had cancer; however, I can talk to you about strokes because my friends have had one and I had one. I thank God daily I'm still alive. I don't want to just have life; I want to have life more abundantly. This is where CNS comes in. I believe all things work together for the good and those who love the Lord and called according to His purpose. Romans 8:28 (NIV 2011) I am at CNS for a reason. I'm not at CNS just to learn how to walk again. I am a light. As of today, I can walk now. In fact, I take 8,000 steps each day (approximately 3.5 miles).

However, I'm still at CNS for other reasons. I need therapy in other areas and I have friends that are not walking. They experience the hope of Jesus when they see me walking over 3 miles each day. Some of the patients might not understand but I'm there to also articulate the hope they are experiencing as they go down the road of recovery.

I don't really know how much longer I will be at CNS receiving therapy; however, I do know I'm not in a hurry to leave until I'm healed and doing 1,000. Meanwhile, I will continue to allow my light to shine and put it on a stand so other patients may see it and benefit from my light. I figure it's not just about me. It's about how God can work through me to will and act according to his purpose. I am just a vessel playing my role so that the Kingdom of God will be enhanced and extended. When my work is done at CNS, I will be prepared for my next assignment.

"No one after lighting a lamp puts it in a cellar or under a basket, but on a stand, so that those who enter may see the light". Luke 11:33 (NIV 2011)

## A Mosquito

One day it was about 8:00 pm, almost dark. I was standing up admiring the hot weather and a mosquito landed on my leg. During pre-stroke, I would have slapped the mosquito with my hand within 1 second of the mosquito landing. Now, post stroke, I have to get permission from my brain before I make such an impulsive move. My brain had to think about my coordination and my balance and for now I'm not in a hurry to do anything. Therefore, the mosquito won because I shook my leg and he got a bite then flew away. Therefore, when the question is asked if I am back to a full recovery? The answer is no. This is just one example I'm aware of that I have to make adjustments moving forward. Even though we are 11 months from my stroke, I have made a major recovery. I might not ever fully recover but I'm okay with my progress. I thank God for my progress. I'm okay and I will be okay if I made no more progress. I'm convinced that my God will supply me with all of my needs and I'm really excited about the future.

## The New Normal

On July 30, 2022, I celebrated the 1-year anniversary of having my stroke. I thank God for my healing and recovery. It's obvious to me I am not 100% (maybe 60-75%) after one year and I'm okay with that because I know God is in control. There is a chance I might not ever get to normal, however, with all of the progress I have made and my journey, I praise God for my new normal. If it's God's will, I can take it from here. He has brought me from a long way. I will use my story to give God the glory. How great is thy faithfulness.

# CHAPTER 9

# The New Journey of Life

**AKA New Orleans Trip**

After 19 months of therapy at the Centre for Neuro Skills (CNS), I'm pushing toward the end of my rehabilitation at CNS. My wife invited me to go with her to her sorority, Alpha Kappa Alpha (AKA), regional conference in New Orleans from April 13-15, 2023. I was reluctant to go at first, however I went to support my wife. Since my stroke happened on July 30, 2021, she has been there for me every day, so I played hooky from therapy and went with her. My youngest daughter, Princess, and my oldest grandson, Nathan, drove us to New Orleans, Louisiana. Yvette has been recruiting Princess to become an AKA. It was a very interesting trip. Despite there being over 8,000 AKA's at the conference, I kept my two eyes only on one of them. This was a good time to experience the real world 21 months after having my stroke. It all started at the hotel. We stayed at the Hilton in the French Quarters. On Thursday evening, New Orleans was having a festival at the Riverfront and I wanted us to walk to it so I could get some exercise or physical therapy. I had fun observing new experiences while making new pathways in the brain. I heard good jazz music and I could smell the aroma of marijuana in the air during our walk. Some people were intoxicated so I avoided them running into me while we were walking. Most of the streets and sidewalks were paved with cobblestone so we were very aware of all uneven surfaces. My concentration was on full alert. There were thousands of people at the festival and I also saw people in wheelchairs having a good time. We did not stay too long. I made it to the festival and back to the hotel without falling or needing assistance. It was worth the challenge and a positive experience for me. We walked over two miles and it wore me out. This is all good. Therefore, I didn't have a problem getting to sleep that Thursday night.

Yvette got up early Friday morning to attend the AKA conference. She made certain I was going to be okay during her absence. Since I convinced her I wouldn't leave the hotel, she felt comfortable leaving me behind. I thought to myself, I'm a grown man, 62-years-old and this is not my first trip. I will be okay. Remember I thought this, I did not say this. However, it is my first visit to New Orleans post stroke. Yvette reminded me that breakfast was over at 9:30 a.m. so I made it to breakfast at 9:25 a.m. all by myself.

I noticed everybody was watching me as I was going through the breakfast line to get my breakfast. I guess since it was almost closing time, they were anxious to gather the food and clean up. Or maybe they saw I needed help and they were there to assist me when I asked. Maybe it was a combination of both. After putting my sausage, eggs and French toast on a plate, I tried to get a glass of juice and carry it with my left hand but my left hand started shaking. Not one but two ladies approached me simultaneously to see how they could help. I accepted the help of one, smiled and said thanks. As I was eating my breakfast at a table all by myself, I had a captive audience waiting to serve me. They made certain I ate all I wanted and they didn't try to hurry me up. It was a great feeling knowing I didn't have to tell anyone I had a stroke and they gave me world class service anyway. I reported this world class service to their supervisor later that day. The next morning, Saturday morning I was eager to go to breakfast again all by myself. I could tell they were waiting for me. I made eye contact with one of them and I nodded my head and said good morning then it was on. They were ready to wait on me and they gave me my space at the same time. In other words, I am an independent man and I would like to do some things all by myself. However, if you observe me long enough you might see me asking for help. I'm not handicapped but it might take me more time to do certain things. I was assisted when I asked for help. They continued to give me world class service. I finished my breakfast and went to their supervisor and gave them a high compliment again.

Sunday morning, we started back home to Dallas, Texas. Yvette and I rode in the back seats as usual. My grandson drove us back home and he has a heavy foot. I didn't want to be a backseat driver so I kept my mouth shut. Yvette and I were good because we slept most of the way. After being chauffeured for over 20 months, I have decided no one can drive as good as me so I think, and getting home safely is what really matters. These young people will drive the same with or without us being in the car. I thought about texting Princes to get her nephew to slow down but I decided not to. Despite being a sleep, I could tell the SUV was slowing down and it eventually came to a stop. I reluctantly woke up thinking it was time for a restroom break. The police woman walked to the front passenger window and asked Nathan for his driver license and registration. Even though she was very nice and polite, she ended up giving him a speeding ticket. I had many things on my mind to say, however, I didn't say anything and I still haven't said anything. I noticed his foot was not as heavy after that stop and I assume his wallet is about $300 lighter. This was just a small part of the trip. Post stroke, I have learned experience can be a better teacher than a conversation. My grandson Nathan learned a lesson without me saying a word.

## 45th Class Reunion of 1978

June 3rd 2023 was a great day to fellowship with my classmates from the class of 1978. I had a blast at our 45th class reunion. These people weren't just classmates, they are genuine friends that have supported me from twenty-two months ago when I had my stroke up to the present day. They were so glad to see me and they gave me so much love. I thank God each time I think of them because our friendship has not suffered at all in 45 years. In fact, it has grown stronger than ever since I had a stroke. I never would have thought that to be the case. My friends had nothing but positive things to say about me such as, "I love you," "you have inspired me and so many people," and "you are so positive," are just a few words expressed from their mouths along with kisses and hugs. I would have loved to spend one hour with each one to express my love and gratitude for supporting me during the darkest moments in my life. There was no way I was going to miss this 45th class reunion even after having my stroke. My stroke was not just for me. It has been an opportunity to share with my classmates and friends. God says all things work together for the good to those who love Him and called according to his purpose. Romans 8:28 (NIV 2011) My stroke was not a mistake. It has been an opportunity to share the good news, the good and the bad and the resurrection power of Jesus through my healing. It is an opportunity to help other people get through their pain publicly or privately. Being present at the reunion allowed my classmates to see first-hand how their many prayers, donations, contributions, etc. have been paying off. They even gave me a standing ovation when I first arrived at the reunion.

Where did all of this love come from?

Popularity was a big deal when we were in high school in 1978. Many of my classmates considered me as one of the most popular person in our class; however, I didn't think so. I believed in building relationships with everyone including those that were considered as the unpopular ones. I literally loved everyone and that's how I was raised. Jesus said if you exalt yourself, He would humble you and if you humble yourself, He would exalt you. Matthew 18:4 (NIV 2011) I believe all of my classmates; rich or poor, male or female, smart or not smart, black or white, popular or unpopular remembered their personal relationship with me and they were excited to show their unconditional love and be a blessing to me during this season of my life. I was honored with a level of respect that helped me see God's grace and mercy even during a crisis such as a stroke.

Despite receiving so much attention, I recognized one classmate that had a stroke recently. I spent much of my time trying to understand him as he was talking to me. Unfortunately, his speech was impaired and he had difficulty with processing and speaking his thoughts. I will spend the next few days trying to reach him or his love one so I can get more information on him and see how I could possibly be a help to this family. It's not all about me. It's about how Jesus can work through me to will and act according to His purposes. In other words, the grace and mercy we get from the Lord as we recover from adversity is the same grace and mercy we use to comfort others as they go through their crisis.

## I Am Proud of You

I have spent my entire career building people up. I have worked with students teaching them how to read. I've worked with athletes training them how to play the game of basketball. I have worked with teachers training them how to work with students that cannot read. Five words I used so often with these people were "I am proud of you". I know these words are supposed to be encouraging, however, you never understand the power of these words until someone says it to you. Not only does it make you feel like you are a winner but it also makes you want to keep on and do better than what you've done before. It makes you feel like you're on the right path to success. As I go through different phases of my rehabilitation, I hear those five words from several people including my wife, therapists and even strangers. From my perspective, all of it is good. However, it sounds more pleasing to the ears when I hear my wife saying these words. Maybe because she saw me in my most vulnerable state after my stroke and she saw more progress than anyone other than myself. I not only saw progress but I also felt progress. My wife saw me at my best and at my worst: therefore, when I hear her say "I am proud of you ", I am the happiest man in the world. It not only makes my day, but it gives me hope so that I could have life more abundantly.

## The Journey

Early in life when we would take a family trip, I could not wait until we reached our destination. Everybody is so focused on their destination, oftentimes we forget to enjoy the journey. I started out that way with that mindset after having my stroke. I had questions like how long will it be before I go back to work and when will I get back to normal? After meeting patients that were impaired more severely than I was, I recognized I had to regroup and form a new mission. My new mission is to encourage and inspire these patients to get better so I could appreciate the journey. All of us must be transformed. Transformation is always a journey. Do not be conform by the things of this world but be transformed by the renewing of your mind. This was done not only by my words but most importantly by my work ethics. I modeled before them many things including having a positive attitude. I modeled before them how to get out of the wheelchair and learn to walk then learn to run. I tried to be the best patient I could be. The Bible says whatever you do, do it as if you are doing it for the Lord.

I took my eyes off me and got excited when I saw the patients or my friends making progress and I became a cheerleader on the side line. I considered this real joy when I saw my friends talking positive, moving their limbs, walking with a walker, talking or walking. Just as the Lord pours out his kindness to me, He expect me to be kind as I interact with others. Team work really makes the dream work. TEAM-Together Everyone Achieves More.

Daily I spent time having conversations with most of the patients at CNS. In fact, I was late to most of my classes because of people talking to me in the hallway. With one lady about my age, as I conversed with her I would touch her hand and we would celebrate together as she moved her fingers. With another man twenty years younger than me, as I called his name, he would get excited, cry out my name the best way he could as he gave me a fist bump. It is because of these daily interactions; I was able to enjoy my journey. I came to the realization the more I enjoyed the journey, the sooner I would reach what I thought was my destination.

After doing this for over 20 months, my journey is about to end. I'm now doing therapy only three days per week instead of five days. I believe my time here at CNS is coming to an end, probably less than three months, two years after having my stroke. It has been a great journey and I'm looking forward to this continued transformation

CHAPTER 10

# A New Theme: Better Not Bitter

In conclusion, my life is good. I am now better, not bitter. I am doing 1,000. To be honest, I am a better person than I was even before I had my stroke. I have slowed down my role and I have learned how to appreciate life. I am content in all things. I take nothing for granted. There used to be a time when I was afraid to talk to someone in a wheelchair. Not only was I in a wheelchair for several weeks, but I have many friends in a wheelchair that I talk to and encourage on a daily basis. I am able to drive now; however, I chose not to drive at the end of my recovery because I'm home so much more. I now enjoy sitting in my recliner or in the family room for two to five hours talking to my wife with my ADHD self. I have learned how to enjoy life sitting down in one place doing nothing. For 25 years I've had a good marriage, but now since I have slowed down, my marriage is even better. Now I know how to say "no" to people without any apology. People don't wish bad things to happen to them. I did not desire to have a stroke. I would rather not be at CNS hanging out with other impaired patients. My choice would have been different; however, God words say, "Just like the heavens are much higher than the earth, so are His ways so much higher than our ways and so are His thoughts much higher than our thought."

We have finite minds. Despite the fact we try to do good, we still do bad and make poor choices. God is infinite. God is omnipresent. God is omnipotent and God is omniscient. Since He created me in my mother's womb, He knows everything there is to know about me. His goal is to build the best version of me. This takes a form of cutting, shaping and molding. We only can see the now. Since He can see the present and the future, He allows things to happen in our lives that we would never choose. These events could be life changing events such as a stroke. I didn't say He cause it to happen, but He allowed it to happen. Even through this journey, God is still making provisions.

CNS has been a work place for me to become a better Christian and not a bitter person. Since I'm at CNS, I will be an asset and not a liability, a blessing and not a curse. I have every opportunity to grow spiritually and exhibit the fruits of the spirit. Jesus says I am the vine and you are the branches. If you abide in me I will abide in you and you will bear good fruit, apart from me you can do nothing. The fruits of the Spirit are love, peace, joy, kindness, goodness, gentleness, patience, faithfulness and self-control. Galatians 5:19-21 (NIV 2011)

## Love

Love is a choice, not a feeling. It deliberately expresses itself in loving ways and always seeks the welfare of others. Every day I attend CNS, I look forward to spreading love to patients and employees. I love to let my light shine.

### What is Love
*Leroy McClure, Jr.*

> *Does love bring us integrity*
> *Does love keep us apart*
> *Does love come and go*
> *Does love stay in our heart?*
> *Does love know its enemy*
> *Does love know its friend*
> *If love stay in our heart*
> *It will keep us from sin.*
> *Love is like the sun*

*That shine so very bright*
*Why don't we quit hiding?*
*And let love become a part of our life.*
*What if love quit shining?*
*Like the sun above*
*Where would this world be*
*Without a little love?*

## Peace –

The world doesn't offer much peace. Just look around. The world cannot give it because the world doesn't know the One who is peace. But for those who have the Spirit of peace within us, the peace of Christ is possible, no matter our circumstances. The peace I have and the peace I share surpasses all understanding.

## Joy –

This joy I have. The world didn't give it to me and the world can't take it away. Having joy and being happy is not the same. I can have joy in the middle of a storm, but I can't be happy in the middle of a storm. May the God of hope fill you with all joy and peace as you trust in him, so that you may overflow with hope by the power of the Holy Spirit. Roman 15:13

## Kindness/Goodness -

The characteristics of "kindness" and "goodness" are closely related. Together they present the picture of one who not only possesses moral goodness and integrity, but also generously expresses it in the way they act toward others. I love expressing kindness to new patients as they go through a storm while giving them hope.

## Gentleness -

Let your gentleness be evident to all. The Lord is near." - Philippians 4:5 (NIV 2011)

Closely linked to humility, gentleness is grace of the soul. It is not weakness, but instead it is strength under control.

Gentleness, being the opposite of self-assertiveness and self-interest, is also a key ingredient in unity and peace within the body of Christ (Ephesians 4:2).

## Patience-

We don't see much patience in the world today, not even in the church. Maybe part of the reason is our fast-paced, want-it-now culture or destination oriented. But Christians have everything we need to be patient because we have the Holy Spirit living in us. I don't know if I will ever have a full recovery. My goal is to be patient with the Lord as he renews my strength and keep me right in the center of his will.

## Faithfulness

GOD has been faithful to me during the entire process. Great is thy faithfulness!

All my life God has been so faithful. All of my life He has been so good. With every breath that I am able, I will sing the goodness of God.

His master replied, 'Well done, good and faithful servant! You have been faithful with a few things; I will put you in charge of many things. Come and share your master's happiness!'"- Matthew 25:21

To be "faithful" is to be reliable or trustworthy. For the Christian, this is faithfulness specifically to the Savior who redeemed us. Christian faithfulness therefore, is continued and consistent submission and obedience to the same Spirit who provides the ability for us to be faithful.

## Self-Control -

In Galatians 5:19-21. Those of us with the indwelling Holy Spirit have the strength to control our sinful desires, to say "no" to our flesh. Self-control gives us the power to say "yes" to the Spirit and foster a beautiful, bountiful harvest of spiritual fruit. As I wait for complete healing, I wait on the Lord. We all know how difficult waiting is during time of illness. However, God can use our situation to develop the virtues He desires in our lives. When I was well, it was like driving 100mph. You only get a glimpse of what you pass by. When you are going slow or in a wheelchair, you get a full picture of everything. Not only do you learn to be more grateful and more concerned about others, but you also learn to do more with less. Little things become big things.

Youth grow tired and weary but young men may stumble and fall but those who wait upon the Lord will renew their strength. They will soar on the wings like an eagle. They will run and not grow weary and they will walk and not faint. I give God the glory. How great is thy faithfulness.

In closing, after getting out of my comfort zone going to New Orleans, driving, grilling food, etc., I can truly say that life is good, I am better not bitter. All of my experiences have been invigorating. It was a blessing for me to get out and go places other than going to church and to rehabilitation. All of things that have occurred in my life since my stroke has taught me that a new quality of life is obtainable and certainly doable. I am looking forward to enjoying life and have life more abundantly long after my rehab days are behind me. I'm looking forward to this continued transformation.

# REFERENCES

n.d. Accessed July 12, 2018. https://www.merriam-webster.com/.

2023. "About Stroke." Centers for Disease Control and Prevention. Cent . May 4. Accessed August 10, 2023. https://www.cdc.gov/stroke/about.htm.

Coelho, Paulo. 2021. The Lesson of the Butterfly. Accessed June 21, 2023. https://paulocoelhoblog.com/2007/12/10/the-lesson-of-the-butterfly/.

n.d. Know Stroke. Accessed August 10, 2023. https://www.ninds.nih.gov/health-information/public-education/know-stroke#:~:text=Each%20year%20in%20the%20United,each%20decade%20after%20age%2055.

2011. Life Application Study Bible. New International Version. Tyndale House Publishers. Accessed July 25, 2017.

Rodgers, Brenda. 2022. What Does It Mean to Have Abundant Life? June 9. Accessed August 10, 2023. https://www.ibelieve.com/faith/what-does-it-mean-to-have-abundant-life.html.

Swindoll, Charles. 2022. Swindoll's Ultimate Book of Illustrations and Quotes: Over 1,500 Ways to Effectively Drive Home Your Message. Nashville, Tennessee: Thomas Nelson Publishers. Accessed August 10, 2023.

www.ingramcontent.com/pod-product-compliance
Lightning Source LLC
LaVergne TN
LVHW020444070526
838199LV00063B/4845